Environmental Education

Environmental Education

JAGDISH CHAND
Former Deputy Director of Education and
Executive Director of the Delhi Bureau of Textbooks,
Delhi Administration

ANSHAH

Anshah Publishing House

Rs. 950

ISBN: 978-81-8364-098-5

2026 Impression

Environmental Education

Published by:
ANSHAH PUBLISHING HOUSE
LG 18-19, Pankaj Central Market,
IP Ext., Patparganj, Delhi 110092
11 47322068; 9650028065, 9810522367
info@shiprapublication.com
www.shiprapublication.com

Preface

The theme of the book acquires a special significance in the present day context and has been made part of curriculum for students of education in number of universities. The three themes — Values, Environment and Human Rights, were published in a combined volume in 2005 by Shipra Publications, but keeping in view demand and requirements of the market and students, publishers approached us to bring out each theme separately also and the proposal gladly accepted. I hope users will take its advantage.

Author has made use of various reports, publications, document — primary and secondary sources to make this book students' friendly and express thanks to their authors and publishers. Utmost care has been taken while compiling this book, and regret if there is any omission. It is suggested that students/teachers must consult reference books or encyclopedias to study the subject in deep.

Jagdish Chand

Contents

1

Meaning of Environment and Environmental Concerns

CONNECTIVITY WITH THE ENVIRONMENT QUOTABLE QUOTES

The following quotes illustrate the interrelations of environments—

1. Everything is interrelated—the birds, sky, sun, earth, you, me. It is an organic unity. If the sun disappears, so will the trees and the birds, if the birds, and trees disappear, you will disappear. Everything is deeply related to each other.—*OSHO*

2. We depend on nature not only for our physical survival, we also need nature to show us the way home, the way out of our own mind.—*Eckhart* in *'Stillness Speaks'*

3. Modern man has lost connectivity with nature outside and his own nature within. He has not only disturbed the outer ecology but has also ruined his inner ecology. We need to restore the balance in the outer as well as inner ecology—the inner being more important than the outer. The outer is essentially the expression of the inner.
—*Swami Chaitanya Keerti*

4. There is a harmony in the natural world which makes the right thing easy and the wrong thing chaos; the right thing is revealed in being right, not just for now and for us, but for the earth and all those who will inherit it...there are natural principles, if we can discover them, to guide everything men may wish to do with land and water and the life they support. —*Allen Duward, 'Our Wildlife Legacy,' Funk and Wagnalls, New York, 1962.*

5. To defend and improve the environment for the present and future generation has become an imperative goal for mankind. —*Declaration of the United Nations Conference on Human Development, Stockholm, 1972.*

6. The environmental crisis is an outward manifestation of a crisis of mind and spirit. There could be no greater misconception of its

meaning than to believe it to be concerned only with endangered wildlife, human-made ugliness and pollution. These are part of it but more importantly, the crisis is concerned with the kind of creature we are and we must, become in order to survive.—*Coldwall, Lynton K. 'Citizens and the Environment Case Studies in Popular Action'* Indiana University Press, Bloomington, 1976.

7. In nature there is enough for everyone's need, but too little for everyone's greed.—*M.K. Gandhi*

8. We shall never understand the natural environment until we see it as a living organism.—*Paul Brooks*

9. We abuse land because we regard it as a commodity belonging to us. When we see land as a community to which we belong we may begin to use it with love and respect.—*Aldo Leopold*

10. Conservation in its widest sense brings a peace of mind which is very difficult to define—just walking under trees, among greenery gives you something that you cannot get anywhere else.—*Mariam Rothschild*

11. Forests are mothers of rivers.—*Sunderlal Bahuguna*

12. Ecology is permanent economy.—*Sunderlal Bahuguna*

13. We don't have a society if we destroy the environment. —*Margaret Mead*

14. Environment is everything that isn't me.—*Albert Ainstein*

15. The environment movement has got to re-educate people. —*Anita Roddick*

16. A forest is a perfect example of the law of return in action. —*Richard St. Baker*

17. Pollution is nothing but the resources we are not harvesting. We allow them to disperse because we have been ignorant to their value. —*R. Buckminster Fuller*

18. Serious pollutants do not respect national boundaries.—*James E. Carrol*

19. Conservation is still in the horse and buggy state while extinctions are happening at the speed of an Exout Missile.—*Geral Durrell*

20. You may forgive noise but your arteries never will.—*Samuel Rosen*

21. Development is the best contraceptive.—*Dr. Karan Singh*

22. Nothing is more likely to lead Threat from H-bomb war than the threat of universal destitution through over population.—*Bertrand Russell*

23. A Nation's wealth, its real wealth, can be gauged by its tree cover..—*Richard St. Barbe Baker*

MEANING OF ENVIRONMENT

In a broader sense, environment is everything that surrounds human beings or it constitutes whatever is present around him, above the land, on the surface of the earth and under the earth.

Environment may be defined as conditions or circumstances that surround an organism.

Environment could be a combination of external or cultural, economic, educational, physical, religious and social conditions that affect growth and development of an organism. In the words of Albert Einstein, "Environment is anything that isn't me.

According to Wordsworth, "The environment is everything that affects the individual except his genes."

Douglass and Holland define environment as, "Environment is a word which describes, in the aggregate, all of external forces, influences and conditions which affect the life, nature, behaviour and the growth, development and maturation of living organism."

For all practical purposes, we have treated environment as the representative of physical components of the earth wherein man in an important factor who is influencing and is being influenced.

COMPONENTS OF THE ENVIRONMENT

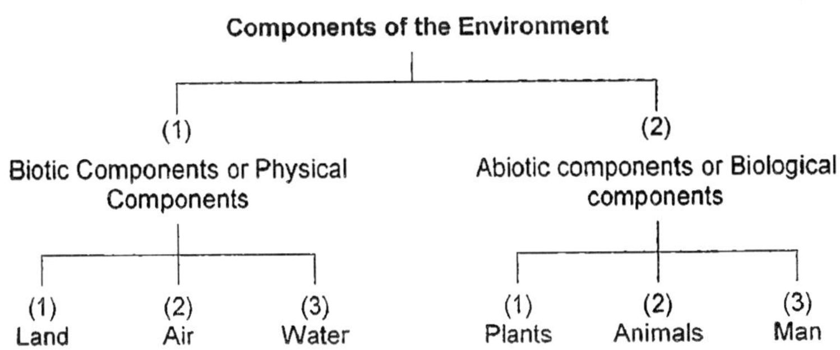

On the basis of physical characteristics, the physical environment is subdivided into the following three broad categories:

(a) *Atmosphere*—gaseous envelope on earth.
(b) *Hydrosphere*—the aquatic portion of biosphere like streams, rivers, ponds, oceans and all water bodies.

(c) *Lithosphere*—the solid portion of earth like land masses, rocks and mountains.

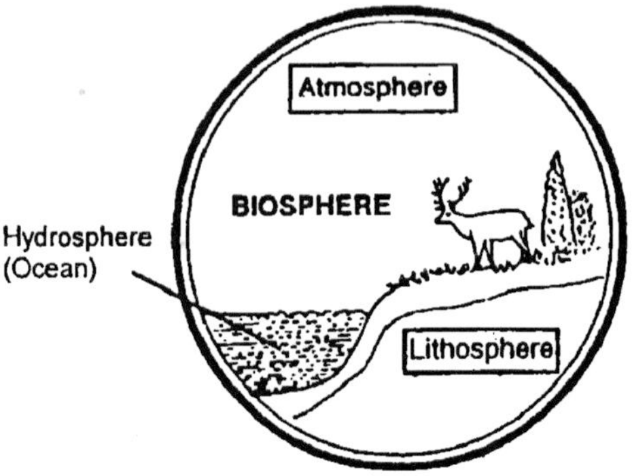

Fig. 1.1: Biosphere

The biological components of the environment consist of plants (flora) and animals (fauna) including man as an important factor.

CHIEF CHARACTERISTS AND ELEMENTS OF ENVIRONMENT

- The term environment not only includes air, water and land but also other *physical surroundings* like buildings, open spaces, land etc., and the *living organisms* like plants, animals and human beings with whom one interacts.
- Environment has a strong influence on the living organisms and in turn the living organisms affect and alter the environment. In fact, they both interact, influence each other and maintain a balance in nature.
- Environment can be defined as a sum total of all *biotic* (living) and *abiotic* (non-living) factors that surround and influence an organism.
- Environment has various components, some act as resource and others as regulatory factors.
  - Resource factors......like air, water and land.
  - Regulatory factors......like animals and plants.
- The term environment can be used both at a large scale and small scale.

  At a large scale......Environment of the habitat in which an organism is living. Here it is reflected in the form of regional or global climatic conditions.

At a small scale......Immediate environment of the organism, which may be very different from the habitat. Here it is reflected in the form of local climatic conditions or microclimate.

Spatial and Time Scale of Environment

The term spatial means *space* and *time* scale means time that may vary from minutes to days to years. Different organisms interact with their environment in different spatial and time scale.

Spatial Scale. It refers to the space in which the organisms react with the environment. For example, a bacterium in soil interacts with only a fraction of a space, but a large tree on land interacts with a large volume of air, water and soil.

Time Scale. It refers to the time scale with respect to changes in a day, months or years like: in a day...... it could be diurnal changes, like the changes in environment or in light and temperature during morning and at night.

IMPACT OF ENVIRONMENT IN ITS TOTALITY: NATURAL ENVIRONMENT AND HUMAN ENVIRONMENT

Our natural environment or physical environment i.e., land, air and water is created by nature. Human environment refers to changes that have been made by man on those natural elements. Both natural and human made environment influence our life styles. Our environment determines our characteristic life styles. The one reason why people in different regions live differently is that they have varying influences. The way we dress, make our houses, prepare our food and enjoy leisure are all to a very large degree governed by our environment.

There is so much around us that is natural. The land on which we build on houses, the air we breathe, the rivers that provide us water for drinking and irrigation are all part of our natural environment.

The cave man's lip was totally determined by his natural environment. The cave was his natural habitat. As man progressed, he made tools, discovered metals and started improving his environment. The houses, farms, canals etc., are all examples of man-made environment.

To-day, we are influenced both by our natural environment and man-made environment.

HUMAN INTERACTION WITH ENVIRONMENT

Human interaction with the environment started from the moment he appeared on earth. The early man afraid of lighting, thunder, dense forests and darkness, started worshipping different aspects of nature. His activities or interaction with the environment had very little impact on it. Gradually, he started making radical changes in the environment to suit his needs. The phenomena reached their summit so to say on a work-wide scale in the twentieth century.

The failure to understand the place and role of man in the environment, the absence of elementary knowledge of the biosphere among people in most countries of the world and the booming scientific and scientific revolution created serious imbalance. The modern development of science and technology led too often to a wasteful intensification of the exploitation of natural resources.

'Biosphere in Danger,' 'On the Way to an Ecological Catastrophe,' 'with an Axe at the Tree of Life' and 'Civilization on the way to its Extinction'—these were some of the sensational statesments expressed regarding environmental pollution.

A simplified diagram of this process of man's influence upon the natural environment is given in figure 1.2.

SIGNIFICANT STATEMENTS ON ENVIRONMENT CONSERVATION AND PROTECTION

1. *Ashoka* was the *first ruler* in recorded history to set up *wildlife sanctuaries*.
2. *Venice* is the first city which instituted the *World's first planned* and administered programme of *forest conservation*.
3. *Hippocrates* was the *first* to recognise the problem of *water pollution*.
4. The term 'Ecology' was first used as far back as *1870* by *Ernest Haeckel*.
5. The *elected representatives of the various nations* met at *Bonn* (Germany) for the *first time* to examine the subject of *environment*.
6. The word 'Ecology' is derived from Greek words which mean 'the study of home?
7. *Energy* is lost when one *organism consumes another*.
8. The *eco-system* of *very deep lakes* is biologically the *least productive*.

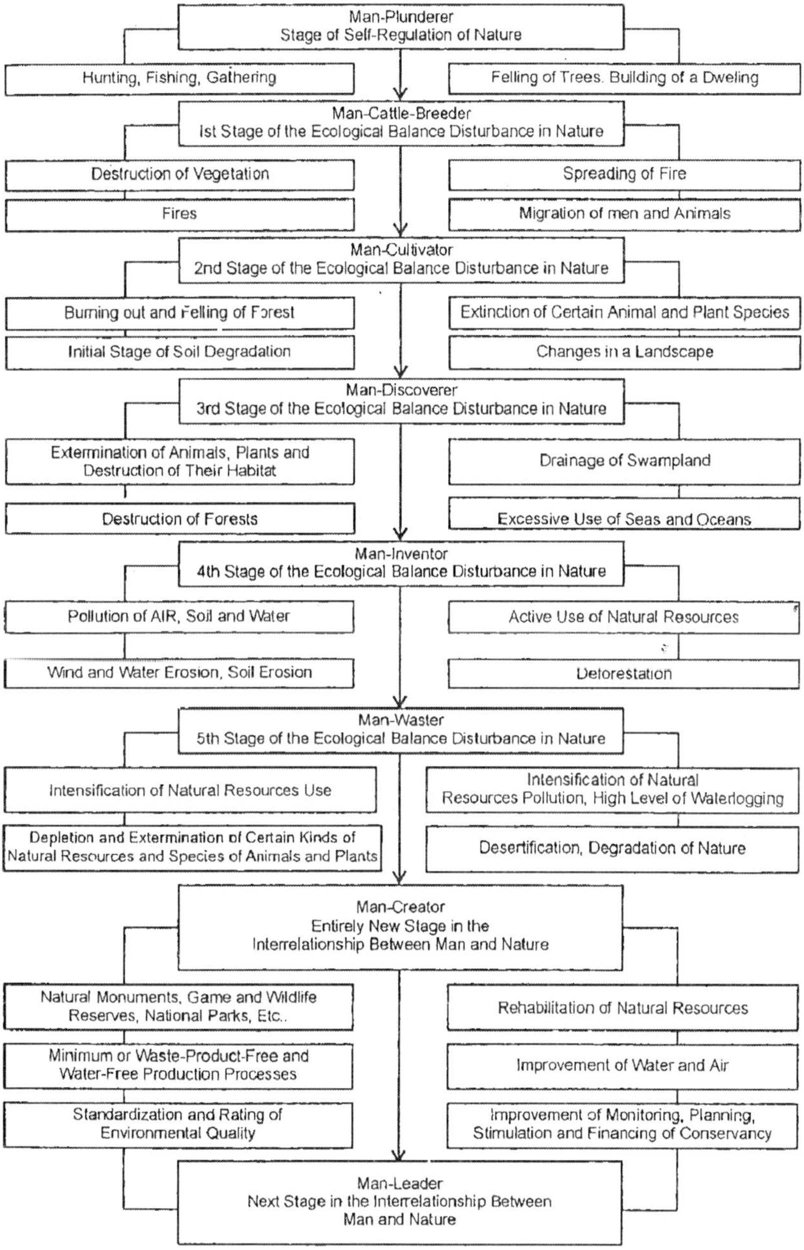

Fig. 1.2: Man-nature Interrelation Stages

Source: *'Living in the Environment': A source book for Environmental Education*, UNESCO, 1985.

9. *Bone narrow* is the first part of the human body to be affected by *nuclear radiation*.
10. *Formaldehyde* was the *first* indoor *pollutant* of which the people became aware.
11. *Corbett National Park* is the *first* national park to be established in *India*.
12. *Geo thermal energy* was *first* used to generate *electricity* in *Italy*.
13. Photochemical smog was *first* noticed in *Los Angeles* in the world.
14. *Alcohol based petrol* as a fuel for automobiles was adopted *first in Brazil*.
15. Alluvial plains ecosystem is biologically the most productive.
16. *Cubat* (Brazil) is often referred to as the 'Valley of Death' as *worst pollution* exists there.
17. The 'Valley of Flowers' is located is *Garhwal Himalayas*.
18. The *worst soil erosion* in the world is taking place at *Himalayan foothills*.
19. *Soil erosion* from wind is the maximum in *Sahel region* (West Africa).
20. *Hiroshima* was the first city to be destroyed by a *nuclear bomb*.
21. An individual on his part can control *pollution* by *controlling* the *consumption* of industrial product.
22. *Plastic household waste* does not *decompose* at all.
23. The *USA* generates the *maximum municipal waste* per head in the world.
24. *Green colour* has become established as a sign of *conservation* and *environment*.
25. The *Hindus* generally consider the '*peepal*' tree sacred and do not cut.
26. The *Hindus* usually use the leaves of the *mango* tree to decorate marriage pandals.
27. *China* has adopted the slogan '*whoever afforests the land will own the trees.*'
28. *Varahamihira*, the renowned *scientist* in ancient India claimed that *termite mounds* were indicators of *ground water*.
29. The *Arthashastra* of Kautilya, the Prime Minister of Chandragupta Maurya, contains rules and regulations for running an *Abhayarnya* (protected forest).
30. *Shivaji* is said to have passed a *law* forbidding *the felling of*

fruit bearing trees for building the ships because it adversely affected the peasantry.

31. The major *source of fuel* in rural India is fuel wood and charcoal.
32. *Indian Prime Minister Rajiv Gandhi* put forward the idea of a 'Planet Protection Fund' to protect the environment of the world at the UN General Assembly.
33. *Marshall McLuhan* coined the term 'global village.'
34. *China* is the *first* country to launch a campaign urging parents to have *only one child* to control population pressure.
35. India is the *first country* in the world to adopt a *national family planning programme.*
36. The noise of *Rock and roll music* is painful to hear and may lead to *loss of hearing.*
37. *Gas Cookers* cause *respiratory illness.*
38. *Air pollutants* enter the body through *respiratory system.*
39. *Cud-chewing* domestic animals release *methane*—a pollutant gas.
40. *Thermal Power Plant* generates fly ash—the *environmental pollutant.*
41. *Carbon monoxide gas* can suffocate living beings to *death.*
42. *Carbon dioxide gas* is mainly responsible for the creation of the *Greenhouse effect.*
43. *Rhine river* was known till recently as 'Europe's Industrial Sewer'.
44. The *diversity of species* is the *lowest* in the *Tundra eco-system.*
45. *Ninety seven percentage* of *water* is present on the *earth* in the forms of *seas* and *oceans*. *Ice-caps and glaciers* lock up *70 per cent* of all *freshwater* available on the earth.
46. *Indira Priyadarshini Vrikshamitra Awards* are given by the Department of Environment, Forest and wildlife, Govt. of India for *contribution to wasteland development* and afforestation.
47. *Soil erosion* led to the *collapse* of the *Maya Civilization* around 900 A.D.
48. The ancient Greek Civilization had passed an *Ordinance* to protect people from noise on account of metal works and keeping roasters.
49. *Salination of the soil* was the main ecological factor that led to the fall of the *Sumerican Civilization* around 2000 B.C.
50. The NCEDC (National Committee on Environmental

Planning and Coordination) advises the Government of India and industry on how to maintain a *cleaner* and *healthier* environment in the country.

51. The *Earth Summit* or Rio Summit which is considered as a landmark in awakening the world to the need for working together for the sake of planet was held in the year 1992.
52. The 'Project Elephant' was set up by the Ministry of Environment and Forests Government of India in 1991-92.
53. The *Decade 1990–1999* was declared as the *International Decade for National Disaster* Reduction.
54. *UNESCO* launched the 'Man and the Biosphere'—a broad-based *ecological programme* in *1971*.
55. The *World Bank* set up an environment department in *1987*.
56. The *World Wide Fund for Nature* was started in *1961*.
57. The *International Union for Conservation of Nature* and *Natural Resources* was set up in *1948*.
58. The *United Nations Environmental Programme* was started in *1972*.
59. *Yaganyalka Samriti* urges man to protect plants and animals for his own *survival* and prosperity.
60. *Delhi* is the first Indian city to adopt *CNG* (Compressed Natural Gas) for public transport.
61. In Kolkata, *human waste* is *recycled* for *fish* farming.
62. In India respiratory and *tuberculosis ailments* are the biggest killers in *Mumbai*.
63. The *first biosphere* reserve was set up in Indian at *Nilgiri*.
64. *Man-eating tigers* are mostly found in *Sunderbans*.
65. The *Chief Justice P.N. Bhagwati* was the first person in India to suggest the setting up of *environmental courts* to deal exclusively with crimes relating to environment.

ENVIRONMENTAL DISEQUILIBRIUM (IMBALANCE) AND ENVIRONMENTAL CONCERNS AND PROBLEMS

In the last few hundred years human population increased tremendously. To cater to the needs of a huge population and on account of rapid and far-reaching advances in science and technology human beings have tried to manipulate the physical environment. In doing so, they have caused environmental imbalance and created a number of environmental problems which are given below:

- Pollution of air, water and land.
- Soil erosion (leading to floods).
- Deforestation (on account of cutting of trees).
- Desertification (as a result of deforestation and soil erosion).
- Giving rise to delicate eco-systems instead of complex and stable eco-systems.
- Landslides and changes in the river direction.
- Extinction of species.
- Depletion of natural resources.
- Thinning of ozone layer and global warming.

Conservation and Protection of Environment

As already observed, various activities of man have led to depletion and degradation of natural resources. For the survival of man, it has become imperative to conserve and protect the environment.

Conservation of environment means the management of use of the biosphere in such a way that it provides optimum benefit to the present generation and also maintains its potential use for the future generation.

Protection of environment implies maintaining the nature as it is or as it might have been before the intervention of human beings or natural forces.

STATE OF ENVIRONMENT IN THE WORLD: A COMPARATIVE STUDY (LAST DECADE OF THE 20TH CENTURY)

S.No.	*Country*	*Indicator*		
		Population	*Forests*	*Pollution*
1.	*Bangladesh*: No primary rain forest left, causing killer floods, 97 per cent of rural dwellers have no sanitation.	×	×	×
2.	*Brazil*: Sixth highest per capita green house omissions. Dropped some deforestation subsidies.	×	×	×
3.	*Canada*: Poor energy efficiency. Concerned over acid rain, but continuous to burn coal without stack control.	√	×	×
4.	*China*: Third highest green house emissions, 9.1 per cent of world total. Heavy forest, loss, choking urban pollution.	√	×	×

(*Contd.*)

S.No	*Country*	*Indicator*		
		Population	*Forests*	*Pollution*
5.	*Congo*: Little safe drinking water. 68 per cent of rain forest scheduled for clearing 5.8 children per woman.	×	×	×
6.	*Costa Rica*: Pioneer in protecting biodiversity and forests. 3.3 children per woman.	×	√	√
7.	*Czechoslovakia*: Highly polluted cities and water. 90 per cent of all wells in the countryside are contaminated.	√	×	×
8.	*Egypt*: Hefty pesticide subsides cause chemical-related deaths and pollution, 4.4 children per woman.	×	×	×
9.	*Ethiopla*: Loses 1 billion tons of topsoil per year to over cultivation. Little clean water 7.5 children per woman.	×	×	×
10.	*France*: Reliance on nuclear power cuts greenhouse emissions (1.5% of world total). 1.8 children per woman.	√	√	√
11.	*Germany*: Acid rain decimating forests 35,000 abandoned toxic-waste sites. High energy efficiency.	√	×	×
12.	*India*: Fifth highest greenhouse emissions. Almost all primary rain forest gone. 3.9 children per woman.	×	×	×
13.	*Indonesia*: 10,000 miles of coral reef being destroyed. Pilot project to protect species-rich wetlands.	√	×	×
14.	*Israel*: Pioneered solar energy and desert agriculture. 2.9 children per woman.	√	√	√
15.	*Italy*: Severe pollution of Adriatic. Energy efficient. 1.3 children per woman. Dumped toxics in Nigeria.	√	√	×
16.	*Japan*: Fourth highest greenhouse emissions. Traffics in endangered wildlife. Energy efficient.	√	×	√
17.	*Kenya*: Little safe drinking water outside cities. Trying to save wildlife. 6.7 children per woman.	×	×	×
18.	*Madagascar*: Huge deforestation rate. Little safe drinking water. 6.6 children per woman.	×	×	×

(Contd.)

S.No.	Country	Indicator		
		Population	Forests	Pollution
19.	Malaysia: Huge deforestation rate, mostly for export, to Japan. Has lost half its wetlands in last.	×	×	√
20.	*Mexico*: Horrible air and water pollution. Clears 1.5 per cent of fast-disappearing forests per year.	×	×	×
21.	*Nigeria*: Complete deforestation expected by 2000. Little safe water outside cities. 6.5 children per woman.	×	×	×
22.	*Norway*: Waterways and forests harmed by acid rain, poor commercial energy efficiency.	√	×	√
23.	*Philippines*: Severe deforestation causes killer floods and will leave no virgin forest by 2010.	×	×	×
24.	*Poland*: Extremely polluted. Dumps 20 million tons of toxic waste every year into unregulated sites.	√	×	×
25.	*Saudi Arabia*: A leading opponent of climate treaty. 7.1 children per woman.	×		×
26.	*Thailand*: Lost 45 per cent of forest from 1961 to 1985. Lead poisoning rampant in Bangkok's children.	√	×	×
27.	(ex.) *U.S.S.R.*: Second highest greenhouse emissions, 13.6 per cent of total. Tons of toxics dumped on land and sea.	√	√	×
28.	*United Kingdom*: Has led fight for climate treaty. Improved energy efficiency. 30 per cent since 1970.	√	√	×
29.	*United States*: Highest greenhouse emissions, 17.8 per cent of world total, Subsidizes deforestation.	√	×	×
30.	*Zaire*: Among 25 worst nations in providing safe drinking water. 6.1 children per woman.	×	×	×

Note: √ = good; × = bad.

Source: '*Newsweek*.'

TEACHING-LEARNING STRATEGY FOR EXPLAINING THE HUMAN INTERACTION WITH ENVIRONMENT

The strategy of explaining the human interaction with

environment may be explained in terms of Bloom's taxonomy of objectives–cognitive, affective and psychomotor.

I. Knowledge (Cognitive)

1. To enable the students to understand to inter-relationship between man and natural environment.
2. To enable the students to identify major concepts and terms like migration, emigration, immigration and density of population etc.
3. To enable the students to understand the reasons for uneven distribution of population in different regions of the world.
4. To enable the students to acquaint themselves with the growth trend in population.
5. To enable the students to understand the relation between population and environment.
6. To enable the students to understand the impact of the changing needs of man on environment.
7. To enable the students to understand the impact of Industrial Revolution on environment.
8. To enable the students to compare ecological balance and efficiency in the past with that of the present.
9. To enable the students to distinguish between birth rate and growth rate of population.
10. To enable the students to understand the different ways of making the optimum use of food resources.
11. To enable the students to understand the significance of having better understanding among the nations of the world for meeting food shortage.
12. To enable the students to identify the major type of human activities.
13. To enable the students to understand energy crisis.
14. To enable the students to understand the reasons for the depletion of resources.
15. To enable the students to classify resources between renewal and non-renewal.

II. Interests and Attitudes (Affective)

1. To develop positive interests regarding environmental issues among students.
2. To enable the students to appreciate that growing population

is likely to pose several threats to the standard of life and living.

III. Skills (Psycho-motor)

1. To develop the skill of the students to read population maps.
2. To develop the skill of the students to prepare map showing areas of uneven population.
3. To develop the skill of preparing posters indicating the harmful effects of environmental pollution.

Teaching-Learning Activities

1. The entire lesson would revolve round a table containing comparative indicators of development with respect to developed and developing countries.
2. Illustrations showing interrelations between man and environment will be displayed.
3. Narration interspersed with questions.
4. Project work on environmental and population themes.
5. Debate on various aspects of environmental and population control.
6. Preparation of thrusts indicating causes leading to overpopulation and degradation of environment.

BRIEF HISTORY OF ENVIRONMENT PLANNING (PRESERVATION AND PROTECTION) IN INDIA

Environment in the Indian Constitution

The original Constitution of India did not include environment in the Directive Principles of State Policy. It was not mentioned in any of the three lists of subjects i.e., the Central List, State List and the Concurrent List.

The Constitution (Forty-Second Amendment) Act 1976, led to the insertion of *Article 48A—"Protection and Improvement of environment and safeguarding of forest and wild life'*—The State shall endeavour to protect and improve the environment and to safeguard the forests and wildlife of the country."

Apart from this, a new provision in the form of "*Fundamental Duties*" as *Article 51A* was also incorporated by the 42nd Constitutional Amendment, sub-clause (g) which states, "It shall be the duty of every citizen of India to protect and improve the natural environment including forests, lakes, rivers and wildlife and to have compassion for living creatures."

Environment was put on the world political map in the Stockholm UN Conference on the Human Environment in 1972.

In the same year i.e., in 1972, a National Committee on the Environmental Planning and Coordination was set up by our late Prime Minister Mrs. Indira Gandhi. The objective of the Committee was in line with the recommendations of the Stockholm Conference i.e., to identify and investigate the problems of conserving and improving the Human Environment in India especially in the context of excessive population growth and the deleterious effect it causes on the economic development and social fabric of the country and eroding the base for future generations.

In February 1980, another Committee (Tewari Committee) was set up to review and recommend legislative and administrative measures for ensuring environmental protection. On the recommendations of this Committee, the Department of Environment was set up in November 1980 which in January 1985 became the Ministry of Environment and Forests, located in Paryavaran Bhawan, CGO Complex, Lodhi Road, New Delhi. Its mandate covers the following:

(a) Environmental Laws and Policy
(b) Pollution-Monitoring and Control
(c) Survey and Conservation of Natural Resources
(d) Management and Conservation of Forests and Wildlife
(e) Promotion of Environment Research
(f) Environmental Education, Awareness and Information
(g) International Cooperation.

International Cooperation

The Ministry of Environment and Forests functions as a nodal agency for United Nations Environment Programme (UNEP), South Asia Cooperation Environment programme (SACEP), International Centres for Integrated Environment Programme (ICIMOD), International Union for Conservation of Nature and Natural Resources (IUCN) and various other international agencies, regional bodies and multilateral institutions. The Ministry also functions as the nodal agency and participates actively in international agreements relating to environment such as the Convention on

International Trade in Endangered Species, Convention on Wetlands of International Importance, Convention (1985) for the Conservation of Migratory Species of Wild Animals, Vienna, Convention for the Protection of the Ozone Layer [Montreal Protocol on Substances that Deplete the Ozone Layer (1987)], Convention on Biological Diversity and Climate Change (1992), Kyotto Protocol on climate change (1997) etc. India is also a member of the Basel Convention on Transboundary Movement of Hazardous Substances 1987, and Convention to Combat Desertification (1994) etc. The Ministry also handles bilateral issues and matters, pertaining to multilateral bodies such as Commission on Sustainable Development, UNEP, Environment Support Programme of UNPD (under Country Cooperation Framework-I) and the regional bodies like ESCAP, SAARC and SACEP. In addition, the Ministry also handles the work relating to the National Environment Council and India-Canada Environment Facility.

Ozone Cell

Global efforts to protect the ozone layer started in the early seventies leading to the adoption of the Vienna Convention on Ozone Depleting Substances (ODS) in 1985 and the Montreal Protocol in 1987. India acceded to the Montreal protocol, along with its London Amendment in 1992. To meet the country's commitment on ODS phase-out under the protocol and to disseminate information on ozone and ODS, the Ministry has established an Ozone Cell. The Ministry provides custom/excuse duty exemption for ODS phase-out projects and detailed guidelines/procedures have been finalised to grant duty exemption for new investments with non-ODS technologies. A ban has also been imposed on trade of ODS with new parties. The Ozone Depleting Substances (Regulation and Control) Rules, 2000 has also been notified to provide a legal framework for ensuring compliance of the Montreal Protocol.

(*Discussed separately in detail*).

Important Programme for Conservation and Development of Forests

The Social Forestry Programme: It aims at raising, planting and protecting trees with multiple uses like fire wood, fodder and fruits etc., for the rural community.

The Agro Forestry Programme: It aims at reviving an ancient land for farming, forestry and animal husbandry.

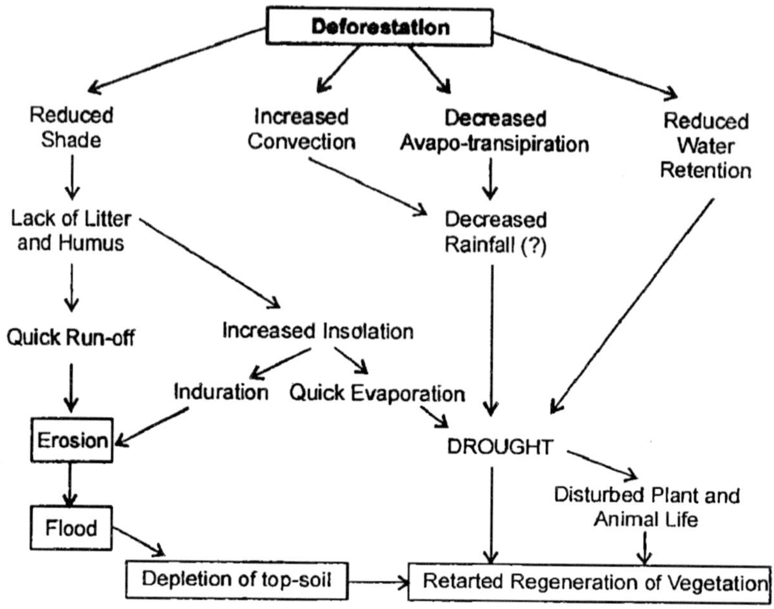

Fig. 1.3: Effects of Deforestation

The Urban Forestry Programme: It aims at planting trees for aesthetic purposes in urban settlements. It also plants flower and fruit trees on the road-side, looks after private compounds and vacant lands.

CHIPKO MOVEMENT

Apart from government programmes, several people's movements like *Chipko movement* in Tehri Garhwal area in Uttaranchal and strong agitation to construct hydroelectric project in the Silent Valley region have protected precious forest wealth.

Chipko movement is considered one of the most effective grass-roots movements to have arisen since the UN Conference on the Human Environment (Stockholm, 1972), because while the capitals of the industrialised countries became centres for discussions on the environment, in a little village lost in the Himalayas a form of non-violent direct action was begun which has spread all over India and today is an example for the rest of the world.

"Chipko" means to embrace (trees) and is the name given to the form of resistance adopted by the Movement with the object of protecting the forests. In India forests are the basis for the subsistence of rural and especially mountain villages, since they provide food, fuel and fodder, etc., play a crucial role in soil conservation, and are source of clean water.

Returning to the teachings of ancestral Hindu wisdom, the Chipko Movement has transformed the industrialist vision of the forest as a producer of wood, resin and currency (from exports) into a new (and at the same time ancient) vision according to which the forest gives us clear air, water and soil, which form the basis of life.

The Chipko movement emerged in the autumn of 1972, after Swami Chidanandji spread the message of the Stockholm Conference and the Sarvodaya Brotherhood started its fight for the community rights to the forest.

The confrontation with the power of the state arose when 50 ash trees in the Mandal forest were allotted to a company manufacturing sports equipment at the same time as the peasants were refused their request to cut down a tree on forestry land to make yokes. On 23 April 1973 they held a demonstration in the forest and the company refrained from cutting the trees down. This kind of demonstration was repeated in other valleys and that was the start of a new form of non-violent resistance, which spread from village to village through the efforts of people like Sunderlal Bahuguna, a Gandhian activist and philosopher who made the 8,870 km march from Kashmir to Kohima speading the message of resistance.

FIRSTS IN ENVIRONMENT ISSUES IN INDIA (ACTS AND POLICIES)

1. The first National Forest Policy was formulated in India in 1952.
2. The Water (Prevention and Control of Pollution) Act came into operation in India in 1974.
3. Air Pollution Control Act in India was promulgated in 1982.
4. The Wildlife (Protection) Act came into operation in India in 1972.
5. The Environment Protection Act was enforced in India in 1986.

6. The Forest Conservation Act in India was passed in 1980.
7. The Department of Environment, Government of India was set up in 1980.
8. The Department of Non-Conventional Energy Sources was set up in 1982.
9. The Project Tiger was launded in India in 1973.
10. The Central Ganga Authority was constituted into guide and over see the environmental issues in 1985.
11. The 'Project Elephant' was set up in Indian 1991–92.

ENVIRONMENT INSTITUTES AND THEIR LOCATIONS IN INDIA

S. No.	*Institute*	*Place of Location*
1.	Asian Elephant Research and Conservation Centre	Bangalore
2.	Central Soil and Water Conservation Research Centre	Dehradun
3.	Centre for Environmental Education	Ahmedabad
4.	Centre for Science and Environment	New Delhi
5.	Centre for Environmental Studies	Chennai
6.	C.P. Ramaswami Aiyer Environmental Education Centre	Chennai
7.	G.B. Pant Institute of Himalayan Environment and Development	Almora
8.	Indian Grassland and Fodder Research Institute	Jhansi
9.	Indian Institute of Forest Management	Bhopal
10.	Industrial Toxological Research Centre	Lucknow
11.	National Environmental Engineering Research Institute	Nagpur
12.	National Institute of Occupational Health	Ahmedabad
13.	National Museum of Natural History	New Delhi
14.	Office of the 'Campaign for Clean Ganga	Varanasi
15.	The Pollution Control Research Institute	Haridwar
16.	Salim Ali Centre for Ornithology	Coimbatore

SOME PROMINENT ECOLOGISTS AND CONSERVATIONALISTS

1. *Anil Aggarwal*: He believes that the only way to attack the problem of deforestation is to create a system within the society which will then feel that growing and supporting trees is crucial to its own survival. Founder of the Centre for Science and Environment in New Delhi.
2. *Barbara Ward*: An eminant writer of thought providing books on environment. '*Only One Earth*' is the most popular book authored by her.

3. *Madhav Gadgil*: He has done pioneering work by linking biodiversity and the needs of the communittees and especially the poor people.
4. *Menaka Gandhi*: A crusader for animal rights in India has served as Minister at the Centre for many years.
5. *M.C. Mehta*: A Supreme Court Lawyer, he has advocated the creation of appropriate environmental laws in India.
6. *Rachel Carson*: She is a biologist and an environmentalist known for her book '*Silent Spring*.'
7. *Salim Ali*: A renowed bird—watcher.
8. *Sunderlal Bahuguna*: A leading environmentalist considers forests as mothers of river.'

SOME BIOSPHERE RESERVES, NATIONAL PARKS AND WILDLIFE SANCTUARIES IN THE COUNTRY

As of September 2002, the Indian wildlife has been protected in 89 National Parks, 492 Wildlife Sanctuaries and 13 Biosphere Reserves.

National Parks: These are areas strictly reserved for conservation of wildlife (include flora and fauna both). Here any activity of forestry, grazing or cultivation is not permitted.

Wildlife Sanctuary: A sanctuary gives protection to fauna only. Here killing or capturing of any species of wild animals is prohibited. Some activities like harvesting of timber and collection of minor forest products are permitted.

Biosphere Reserves: These are a special category of protected areas wherein people are an integral component of the system. These are natural biomes containing unique biological communities and have variety of wild population of plants and animals. There is a core zone where no human activity is permitted, buffer zone with limited human activity and outermost transition zone where a large number of human activities are permitted.

Some Protected Areas and What are They Famous for

Name of the protected area	*Place*	*Famous for*
National Parks		
Kaziranga National Park	Assam	One horned rhinoceros, ducks, geese, pelican, storks.
Nandankanan Biological Park	Bhubaneswar	Captive breeding of white tigers
Kanha National Park	Madhya Pradesh	Known for wild tigers.
Desert National Park	Thar desert	Famous for Blackbuck, Neelgai, Chinkara, and the great Indian Bustard.
National Botanical Garden	Howrah	Preserved many rare species of plants.
Corbett National Park	Uttranchal	Famous for tigers.
Wildlife Sanctuaries		
Dachigam sanctuary	Kashmir	Only place where Kashmir stag is found.
Bharatpur bird sanctuary	Rajasthan	One of the famous wet-land and water bird sanctuary in the world. The only home of the rare Siberian cranes that migrate to India in winter.
Rann of Kutch sanctuary	Gujarat	Famous for Wild ass, Flamingoes, Star tortoise and Desert fox.
Gir sanctuary	Gujarat	Famous for Asiatic Lion, Chital, Sambhar and Neelgai.
Bandipur sanctuary	Karnataka	Famous for Indian Elephants.
Sanctuary in Madumalai	Tamil Nadu	Famous for Indian Elephants.
Sanctuaries in Annamalai Region	Tamil Nadu	Protect the most biologically rich areas of Shola forests. These include Silent valley. Top slip and Perumbiceulam.
Biosphere Reserve		
Simlipal Biosphere Reserve	Orissa	Famous for Tigers.

TENTATIVE VALUE OF A TREE HAVING A LONG-LIFE

(Neem, Peepal, Banyan, Mango or Jamun)

1.	Generates oxygen worth	Rs. 8.6 lakhs
2.	Greatest air pollution control worth	Rs. 10.5 lakhs
3.	Recycles fertility and soil erosion control worth	Rs. 8.4 lakhs
4.	Creates shelter for birds and other animals worth	Rs. 5.3 lakhs
5.	Provides flowers, fruits, medicines and other	Rs. 4.3 lakhs
	goods worth Total value	Rs. 32.0 lakhs
	Felling of one tree means a net loss of about	Rs. 32.0 lakhs

INTERNATIONAL ENVIRONMENTAL INITIATIVES

The UN has been greatly concerned about environmental issues. Following important actions and measures have been initiated by it.

The United Nations Conference on Environment Stockholm June 1972

The UN Conference was a major event for those concerned with the quality of the environment of the world. This Conference resulted in the creation of the United Nations Environment Programme. It also focused attention on an international environmental education programme.

United Nations Environmental Programme UNEP (1972)

Environment in the modern times was put on the World political map when the UNEP was founded in 1972 for the following objectives:

1. To provide leadership in caring for the environment.
2. To encourage partnership in caring for the environment.
3. To enable nations and people to improve their quality of life without compromising the interests of the future generations.
4. To promote implementation of the environmental dimension of sustainable development.
5. To serve as an authoritative advocate of the global environment.

International Workshop on Environmental Education, Belgrade (1975)

Stockholm Conference on Environment was followed by International Environmental Workshop of Education at Balgrade (Yugoslavakia) in 1975. The workshop listed environmental goals and environmental Education Goals.

Environmental Conference on Environmental Education at Tbilisi (USSR) (1997)

This Conference is considered a landmark in environment education. The Declaration adopted at the Conference proclaimed, "to defend and improve the environment for present and future generations has become an imperative goal for mankind." The Conference also adopted a detailed programme of environmental education. This programme is discussed in relevant chapters.

World Commission on Environment and Sustainable Development (1983)

The Commission established in 1983 by the UN General Assembly aims at bringing about a new understanding and sense of urgency to the new kind of development that would ensure economic well-being of the present and future generations while protecting environmental resources on which all development attends.

Vienna Convention for the Protection of the Ozone Layer (1985) and Montreal Protocol

Under the agreements, developed countries have banned the production and sale of Chlorofluorocarbons a chemical that depletes the ozone layer.

Global Environmental Facility (GEF)

GEF was launched in 1991 to provide funds for conserving biological diversity, addressing global climatic change, reversing the degradation of international waters and phasing out substances that deplete the ozone layer. Funds are also given to stem the pervasive problem of land degradation.

Intergovernmental Panel on Climate Change (IPCC)

IPCC was jointly organised in 1988 by UNEP–WHO (World Meteorological Organisation)

United Nations Framework Convention on Climatic Change

To counter global warning, United Nations Framework

Convention on Climatic change was developed and signed in Rio in 1992.

The Earth Summit Agenda 21 (Discussed Separately)

Kyoto Protocol (1997)

According to this Protocol developed countries are to reduce their collective emission of six greenhouses gases by 5.2 per cent between 2008 and 2012, taking 1990 levels as the baseline.

On 16 February 2005, the Kyoto Protocol entered into force. In the words of UN Secretary-General Kofi Annan said:

"From now on, industrialized countries that are party to the Protocol have a clear obligation to reduce emissions. To do so, they can use the market to trade a new commodity: carbon. The Protocol will also generate resources for developing countries, to help them deal with climate change," he said, while calling on the world community to be bold, to adhere to the Kyoto Protocol, and "to act quickly in taking the next steps."

The Kyoto Protocol's entry into force means that from 16 February 2005:

- Thirty-five industrialized countries and the European Community are legally bound to reduce their combined emissions of six major greenhouse gases during the five-year period 2008-2012 to below 1990 levels.
- The international carbon trading market receives a strong market signal. The Protocol's "emissions trading" regime enables industrialized countries to buy and sell emissions credits amongst themselves; this market-based approach will improve the efficiency and cost-effectiveness of emissions cuts.
- The Clean Development Mechanism (CDM) gets a major boost. It encourages investments in developing-country projects that promote sustainable development while limiting emissions.
- The Protocol's Adaptation Fund, established in 2001, can become operational to assist developing countries to cope with the negative effects of climate change.

The United Nations Conference on Environment and Development: Earth Summit Agenda 21

Agenda 21: The United Nations Conference on Environment and Development (UNCED) held at Rai de Janeiro in 1992 agreed to a global environment and development agenda for the 21st Century called Agenda 21. Agenda 21 is an expression of collective aspirations and commitment of the signatories to push it forward from a statement of hope to a pragmatic blueprint for organising a sustainable society out of the present economically and environmentally inequitable world. The Agenda recognises education as an important instrument of solving environmental problems.

The Agenda 21 takes into account all areas/subjects having bearing on global environment.

Chapter 36 of the Agenda emphasises the role of education in protecting and promoting environment.

Following programmes were suggested:

1. Reorienting education towards sustainable development.
2. Increasing public awareness.
3. Promoting training.

Select Programmes Included in Agenda 21

1. Promoting and protecting human health conditions.
2. Integrating environment and development in decision-making.
3. Protecting the atmosphere.
4. Combating deforestation.
5. Managing fragile eco-systems: combating desertification and drought.
6. Promoting: Sustainable mountain development.
7. Promoting sustainable agriculture and rural development.
8. Conserving of biological diversity.
9. Ensuring environmentally sound management of biotechnology.
10. Protection of the oceans, all kinds of seas, including enclosed and semi-enclosed seas, and coastal areas and the protection, rational use and development of their living resources.
11. Protecting the quality and supply of fresh water resources:

application of integrated approaches to the development, management and use of water resources.

12. Promoting environmentally sound management of toxic chemicals, including prevention of illegal international traffic in toxic and dangerous products.
13. Promoting environmentally sound management of hazardous wastes, including prevention of illegal international traffic in hazardous wastes.
14. Promoting environmentally sound management of solid wastes and sewage-related issues.
15. Undertaking safe and environmentally sound management of radioactive wastes.
16. Developing scientific and technological community.
17. Strengthening the role of farmers.
18. Transferring environmentally sound technology.
19. Using science for sustainable development.
20. Promoting education public awareness and training.

Institutes and Journals on Environment

1. *Natural History Journal*
2. *Bhagirath*
3. *Ecology Law Quarterly*
4. *Environmental Review*
5. *Environmentalist*
6. *Environmental Conservation*
7. *Indian Journal of Environmental Health*
8. *Environmental Health Perspectives.*

Institute/Organisation which Brings out the Journal on Environment

- American Museum of Natural History
- Central Water Commission of India
- California University (USA)
- American Society for Environmental History
- Institute of Environmental Sciences, London
- Foundation for Environmental Conservation, Switzerland
- National Environmental Engineering Research Institute, Nagpur (India)
- National Institute Environmental Health Sciences, USA.

Major Internationl Institutions Relating to Environmental Issues

1. World Resources Institute, Washington DC
2. Centre for International Environmental Information, New York
3. Scientific Committee on Problems of Environment, Paris
4. World Commission on Environment and Development, Geneva
5. International Council for Environmental Law, Bonn
6. United Nations Environmental Programme (UNEA), Nairobi
7. International Institute for Environment and Development, London

2

Meaning, Aims, Objectives, Scope and Principles of Environmental Education

MEANING AND DEFINITION OF ENVIRONMENTAL EDUCATION

As observed in *Encylopaedia of Educational Research* edited by Harold E. Mitzel (1982), "Defining 'environmental education' is not an easy task, unlike other curriculum areas the specific content of environmental education has never been well defined. It is universally agreed, however, that environmental education should be interdisciplinary, drawing from biological, sociological, anthropological, economic, political and human resources. It is also agreed that a conceptional approach to teaching environmental education is the best." Some of the definitions of environmental education are given here to have a wider perspective of this concept.

1. "Environmental education is the process of recognising values and clarifying concepts in order to develop skills and attitudes necessary to understand and appreciate the inter-relatedness among man, his culture and his biophysical surroundings. Environmental education also entails practice in decision-making and self-formulation of a code of behaviour about issues concerning environmental quality." (*International Union for the Conservation of Nature and Natural Resources Commission of Education, International Working Meeting on Environmental Education in the School Curriculum*, Paris, UNESCO, 1970).
2. Environmental education is the educational process which deals with man's relationship with his natural and man-made surroundings, and includes the relation of population, pollution, resources allocation and depletion, conservation,

transportation, technology and urban and rural planning to the total human environment in the United States Public Law 91-516. (*The Environmental Education Act, 1970*)

3. Environmental education involves teaching about value judgements and the ability to think clearly about complex problems—about the environment—which are as political, economical, and philosophical as they are technical. (*Proceedings of the organisation of American States Conference on Education and the Environment, 1971*).
4. "Environmental education is a way of implementing the goals of environmental protection. Environmental education is not a separate branch of science or subject of study. It should be carried out according to the principle of lifelong integral education." (Finnish National Commission for UNESCO *Report of the National Seminar on Environmental Education, 1974)*.
5. Environmental education, properly understood, should constitute a comprehensive lifelong education, one responsive to changes in a rapidly changing world. It should prepare the individual for life through an understanding of the major problems of the contemporary world, and the provisional of skills and attributes needed to play a productive role towards improving life and protecting the environment with due regard to ethical values." (*The First Intergovernmental Conference on Environmental Education*, Tbilisi, 1977.)
6. "Environmental education is an educational concept which considers the environment as a scientific and aesthetic resource to be used in a lifelong educational process, thus making people knowledgeable and aware of the environment and its problems as well as their own role in environmental conservation, preservation and management."

Living in the Environmen: A Source Book for Environmental Education. UNESCO/UNEP, 1985.

Environmental education implies establishing ecological equilibrium which means proper use and conservation of resources and also control of environment pollution. Environmental education is a process of recognising values and clarifying concepts relating to environment and its problems. The aim is to develop skills and attitudes necessary to understand environment. Environmental Education has been described as education for the environment, education about the environment and education through the environment.

Environmental education is designed to open our eyes to the havoc we have brought on ourselves. Environmental education should enable people learn how hazardous environmental pollution, population explosion and resource depletion could be. The best place to start such learning is school.

Environment Education as a Process

Environmental education should be thought of a process which takes place 'for' and 'in' the environment. By 'for' we mean that the objective of all education, and of environmental education in particular, is to enable the individual to fulfill his potentialities and aspirations while acquiring a sense of responsibility and commitment with regard to the improvement improvement of environmental quality for the benefit of all humanity. 'In' expresses the fact that all resources of the environment itself should be used in the educational experience. It should not be forgotten that environmental education evolves around three central themes, each of which represents a particular stage:

1. education in which the environment represents a means,
2. education concerning the environment, and
3. education of the individual as person living in an environment of a given quality and who is partly responsible for that quality.

Environmental education is a fundamental process through which persons at all possible educational levels (present and future citizens) become aware of, and concerned with, the environmental and its related problems, and acquire the knowledge, skills and determination needed to solve those problems. It is based on eco-development, i.e., scheme of action which is linked with undertakings in virtually every field and which could very well constitute a means of initiating and consolidating a new orientation for human development. In this sense, environmental education is a vast and multi-interdisciplinary pedagogical approach which involves all kinds of institutions and individuals. It is a process which enables us to acquire an understanding of the complex nature of the environment of which we are a part, and to appreciate humanity's dependence on, and responsibility for the environment. It is a means of achieving the goals of environmental management. It is a new educational approach to the relations of people and their environment. It is an experience based education which uses the totality of physical, natural and human resources of a milieu of a learning laboratory.

CHARACTERISTICS OF ENVIRONMENTAL EDUCATION

1. Environmental education is the result of the reorientation and dovetailing of different disciplines and educational experiences which facilitate an integrated perception of the problems of environment.
2. Environmental education is a continuous process.
3. Environmental education is for all age groups.
4. Environmental education caters to all socio-professional groups in the population.
5. Environmental education is a newly created field.
6. Environmental education orients to an environmental issue or problem.
7. Environmental education involves concern for situations that have real consequences for a society.
8. Environmental education is interdisciplinary.
9. Environmental education includes action in relation to the problem.
10. Environmental education aims to clarify values, and in some instances to change them in relation to environment.
11. Environmental education is concerned with the bases for choice between alternatives.
12. Environmental education seeks to develop skills for solving environmental problems.
13. Environmental education seeks alternative solution for environmental situations.

AIMS OF ENVIRONMENTAL EDUCATION

1. To develop constructive attitudes toward the environment, in both the philosophical and programmatical senses, which have not yet become an ingredient in everybody's thinking and acting. (*Final Report: Inter-Governmental Conference of*

Experts on the Scientific Bases for the Rational Use and Conservation of the Resources of the Biosphere, 1968).

2. To develop awareness of and concern about the environment and its associated problems, and to develop knowledge, skills, attitudes, motivations and commitment to work individually and collectively towards solutions of current problems and prevention of new ones (APP. Fensham "*A Report on the Belgrade Conference on Environmental Education, Canberra*, 1976, page 25).
3. To succeed in making individuals and communities understand the complex nature of the natural and the built environments resulting from the interaction of their biological, physical, social, economic and cultural aspects, and acquire the knowledge, values, attitudes, and practical skills to participate in a responsible and effective way in anticipating and solving environmental problems, and the management of the quality of the environment. (*Final Report of Tbilisi Inter-Governmental Conference on Environmental Education, 1977*).

Environmental Education is a Newly Created Field

The conclusions and reports of UNESCO conferences and meetings such as the Belgrade Workshop (1975), the regional meetings held in 1976–1977 in Africa, the Arab States, Asia, Europe and Latin America, as well as several subregional meetings and workshops and the Tbilisi Conference (1977) have helped considerably in clarifying environmental education concepts and in formulating recommendations and proposals for future action.

By its very nature and function, environmental education forms an integral part of society.

Environmental education must insist on the value and necessity of local, national and international co-operation with a view to solving environmental problems. It must be stressed, however, that the most convincing declarations, the most preserving efforts of international (governmental and non-governmental) organisations, are worthless in the absence of a national political commitment. Governments have a crucial role to play in a field in which the most urgent tasks consist in establishing objectives, deciding on strategies and mobilising the vital forces of a nation, its material, human and financial resources, in order to make environmental education an element for the necessary transformation of society.

TBILISI CONFERENCE (1977)—A LANDMARK IN ENVIRONMENTAL CONFERENCE

The first Intergovernmental Conference on Environmental Education, organised by UNESCO in cooperation with the United Nations Environmental Programme (UNEP) was held at Tbilisi in erstwhile USSR from 14 to 26 October 1977. The Conference made important recommendations on the following:

1. Role of environmental education.
2. Objectives of environmental education.
3. Guiding principles of environmental principles.

ROLE OF ENVIRONMENTAL EDUCATION

Environmental education should make individuals and committees understand the complex nature of the natural and the built environments resulting from the interaction of their biological, physical, social, economic and cultural aspects. It should enable them to understand the economic, political and ecological interdependence of the modern world, in which decisions and actions by the different countries can have international repercussions.

Goals of Environmental Education

The goals of environmental education according to Tbilisi Declaration are:

— to foster a clear awareness of and concern about, economic, social, political and ecological interdependence in urban and rural areas;

— to provide every person with opportunities to acquire the knowledge, values, attitudes, commitment and skills needed to protect and improve the environment;

— to create new patterns of behaviour of individuals, groups and society as a whole towards the environment.

OBJECTIVES OF ENVIRONMENTAL EDUCATION

1. *Awareness.* To help individuals and social groups acquire and awareness of and sensitivity to the total environment and its allied problems.

2. *Knowledge.* To help individuals and social groups acquire basic understanding of the total environment and its associated problems.
3. *Attitude.* To help individuals and social groups acquire social values, strong feelings of concern for the environment and the motivation for actively participating in its protection and improvement.
4. *Skills.* To help individual and social groups acquire the skills for solving environment problems.
5. *Evaluation Ability.* To help individuals and social groups evaluate environmental measures and education programmes in terms of ecological, political, economic, social, aesthetic and education factors.
6. *Participation.* To help individuals and social group develop a sense of responsibility and urgency regarding environmental problems to ensure appropriate action to solve those problems.

PRINCIPLES OF ENVIRONMENTAL EDUCATION

The Tbilisi Conference suggested the following guiding principles of environmental education:

1. Consider the environment in its totality—natural and built, technological and social (economic, political, technological, cultural, historical, moral aesthetic);
2. Be a continuous lifelong process, beginning at the preschool level and continuing through all formal and nonformal stages;
3. Be interdisciplinary in its approach, drawing on the specific content of each discipline in making possible a holistic and balance perspective;
4. Examine major environmental issues from local, national, regional, and international points of view so that students receive insights into environmental conditions in other geographical areas;
5. Focus on current and potential environment situations, while taking into account the historical perspective;
6. Promote the value and necessity of local, national, and international cooperation in the prevention and solution of environmental problems;

7. Explicitly consider environmental aspects in plans for development and growth;
8. Enable learners to have a role in planning their learning experiences and provide an opportunity for making decisions and accepting their consequences;
9. Relate environmental sensitivity, knowledge, problem solving skills and values clarification to every age but with special emphasis on environmental sensitivity to the learners own community in early years.
10. Help learners discover the symptoms and real causes of environmental problems;
11. Emphasise the complexity of environmental problems and the need to develop critical thinking and problem solving skills.
12. Utilise diverse learning environments and a broad array of education approaches to teaching/learning about and from the environment with due stress on practical activities and first-hand experience.

These principles indicate that environmental education is a process which inculcates values and elucidates concepts so as to develop those skills and attitudes needed in understanding and appreciating interactions between man and his environment. This education stimulates civic action, decision making and the elaboration of a personal code of conduct with regard to problems concerning eco-development and the quality of life. From the integration of environmental education aspects, formal education will gain a renewed vigour which will open up wider horizons, and non-formal education, whether in the home of the community, will acquire greater responsiveness to social needs. However, since environmental education is innovative in every respect, it implies a reorientation of existing knowledge to real problems and community needs. This necessitates the revision of curricula, teaching methods and certain educational structures, concerning which much remains to be said.

The Tbilisi Conference made evident to all the necessity of developing an education of people for people, since "the protection and enhancement of the environment for present and future generations has become a primordial objective for humanity." If education is to play an essential role in the awakening of environmental consciousness, then it should be noted that the environment has the power to induce education to play this role by obliging it to take into account the diverse existing forces and evolutionary processes. What comes out clearly in the Declaration of Tbilisi Conference is the urgency of 'action in favour of environmental protection,' and, even more the need to place education at its service.

Environment Education for Whom?

The Tbillis Conference considered three categories of those receiving environment education:

1. *The general public*: this education should be provided at every age and at all levels of formal education, for pupils and teachers, and in various non-formal activities, for young people and adults including the handicapped.
2. *Specific occupational or social groups*: this education is focussed on those whose activity and influence have an important bearing on the environment, for instance, engineers, architects, administrators and planners, industrialists, trade-unionists, policy-makers and agriculturalist. Various levels in formal and non-formal education should contribute to this training;
3. *Certain professionals and scientists*: this training, is for those working on specific problems of the environment, such as biologists, ecologists, hydrologists, toxicologists, soils scientists, agronomists, foresters, landscape architects, oceanographers, limnologists, meteorologists and sanitary engineers. It is important that the training of scientists include an interdisciplinary component.

Summing up

Environmental education must insist on the value and necessity of local, national and international co-operation with a view to solving environmental problems. It must be stressed, however, that the most convincing declarations, the most preserving efforts of international (governmental and non-governmental) organisations, are worthless in the absence of a national political commitment. Governments have a crucial role to play in a field in which the most urgent tasks consist in establishing objectives, deciding on strategies and mobilising the vital forces of a nation,

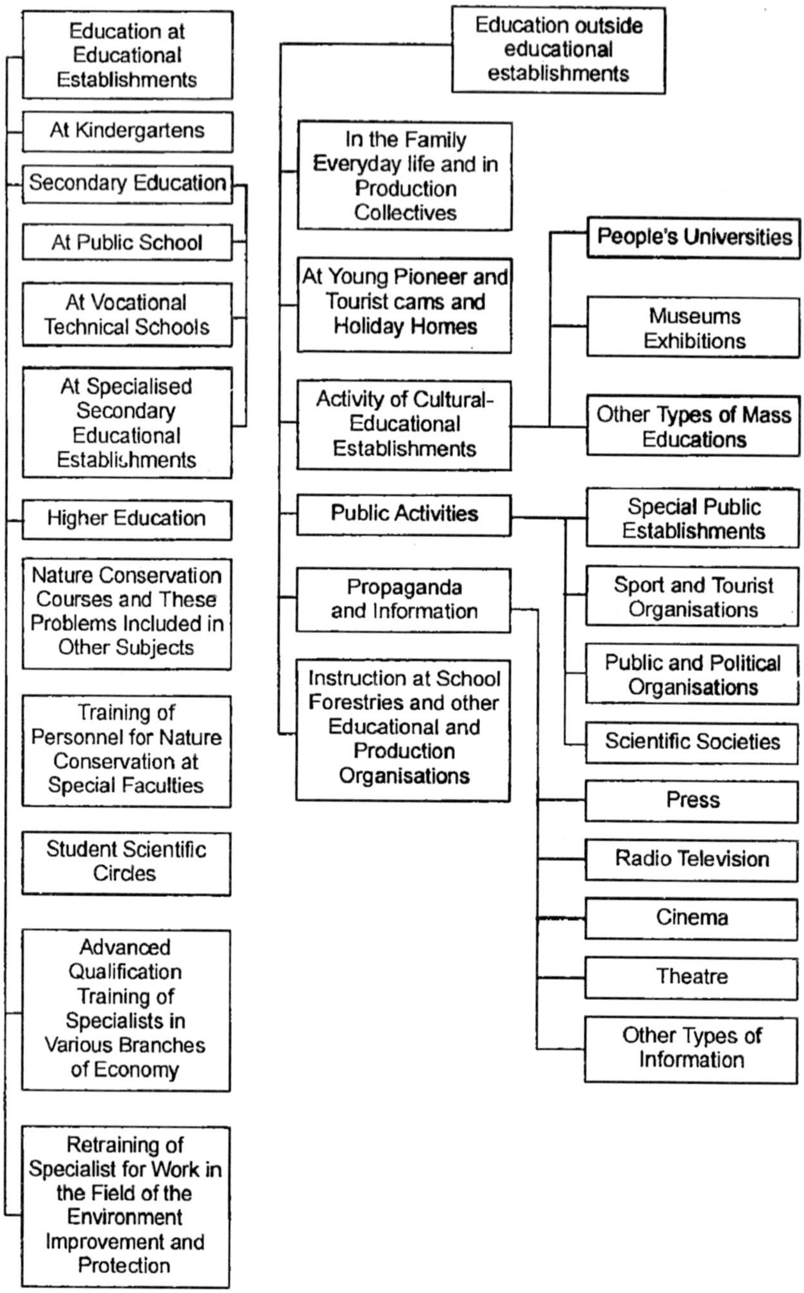

Fig. 2.1: System of Education in the Environmental Field (according to Mitryushkin *et al.*, 1980)

its material, human and financial resources, in order to make environmental education an element for the necessary transformation of society.

To understand correctly the significance and practical relevance of environmental education needs and priorities in a given country, it is essential to know first, how the country itself perceives and takes care of its environment; and secondly, the role and functions of education in the society concerned. The need to elucidate these considerations so as to ensure an adequate understanding of environmental education practices in each country stems from the fact that educators in most countries have to develop courses and teaching methods adapted to local needs and conditions.

SCOPE OF ENVIRONMENTAL EDUCATION

The scope of environmental education is very vast. Broadly, it covers the following elements:

1. Essential knowledge about the Environment.
2. Essential knowledge about the Problems of Environment.
3. Broad based measures towards the Solution of Environment Problems.

Details are given below:

1. Essential Knowledge About the Environment

A. *Structure and Functions of an Eco-system*
   1. Types of Eco-system
   2. Concept of limiting factors.

B. *Energy Flow in the Abiotic Component of the Earth Eco-system*
   1. The earth's ultimate source of energy
   2. Factors affecting energy flow in the earth eco-system
   3. Water cycle, its role in energy flow
   4. Energy transformations and eventual "lost"
   5. Energy from the earth's interior

C. *Energy Flow in the Biotic Component of the Earth Eco-system*
   1. Photosynthesis
   2. Respiration
   3. Food chain and food web
   4. Tropic levels

5. The ten percent law.

D. *Materials Flow in the Biochemical Cycles*
   1. Earth processes, their role in nutrients flow
   2. Water cycle, its role in nutrient flow
   3. The gaseous cycle:
      (a) Carbon cycle
      (b) Nitrogen cycle
      (c) Oxygen cycle.
   4. Sedimentary cycles
      (a) Phosphorus
      (b) Sulphur.
   5. Biological magnification

E. *Population Dynamics*
   1. Population density
   2. Natality, mortality and dispersal
   3. Age structure
   4. Population growth form
   5. Regulation of population size
   6. Natural selection and evaluation.

F. *Human Intervention in Natural Processes*
   1. Human activities that affect energy flow in the earth eco-system:
      (a) Increased combustion and carbon dioxide production
      (b) Smog, soot and other particulate matter
      (c) Ozone
      (d) Concentration of human population, heat sink and wind flow in cities.
   2. Human activities that affect materials flow in the earth eco-system.
      (a) Air pollution
         (i) Carbon monoxide
         (ii) Hydrocarbons
         (iii) Oxides of sulphur
         (iv) Oxides of nitrogen
         (v) Oxidants
         (vi) Other pollutants.
   3. The human eco-system

II. Essential Knowledge about Problems of the Environment

A. *Four Major Dimensions of Environmental Problem*
   1. The physical, economic, and social consequences of environmental problems
   2. The graphical scale of environmental problems
   3. The time scale of environmental problems
   4. The socio-economic systems affected by environmental problems.

B. *Major Causes of Environment Problems*
   1. Rapid population growth
      (a) Food shortage
      (b) Decreasing surface area
      (c) Water shortage
      (d) Energy crisis
      (e) Scarcity of the earth's material.
   2. New problems from science and technology
      (a) Medical technology
      (b) Agricultural technology
      (c) Energy technology
      (d) Food technology
      (e) Materials substitution technology.
   3. New problems from development and industrialisation
      (a) Cost of development
      (b) Development in developing countries
      (c) Increased waste production and pollution
      (d) Cost of pollution.
   4. Concentration of human population (urbanisation)
      (a) Unemployment and poverty
      (b) Concentration of wastes
      (c) High incidence of diseases
      (d) Conflicting land uses.

III. Broad-Based Measures toward the Solution of Environment Problem

1. Control of population growth
   (a) Birth control through education
   (b) Persuasion:
      (i) Family planning
      (ii) Socio-economic measures.
   (c) Use of medical science
      (i) The pill

- (ii) Intrauterine device
- (iii) Abortion
- (iv) Sterilisation.

2. Using science and technology to solve environmental problems
   - (a) Expanding and improving traditional food sources
   - (b) Developing new and unconventional food sources
   - (c) Treatment of malnutrition
   - (d) Pollution abatement:
     - (i) Air pollution abatement
     - (ii) Water pollution abatement.
   - (e) Recycling.
3. Planning human intervention on the natural processes. Broadly speaking following may be the major topics of environmental education:
   1. Purpose and Role of the Biosphere
   2. The Environment and its Elements
   3. Reserve of Natural Resources
   4. Man and Ecological Balance
   5. Atmospheric Exploitation
   6. Conservation and Exploitation of Sand Resources
   7. Conservation and Exploitation of Biotogical Resources
   8. Population Problem
   9. The Environment, Public Health Care and The Food Problem
   10. Environmental and Economic Development
   11. Environmental Management Control
   12. International Cooperation and Environmental Protection. (UNESCO, 1983).

PATTERN OF ENVIRONMENTAL EDUCATION CURRICULUM

The UNESCO Training Workshop on Environmental Education (1980) suggested the following two models:

1. Interdisciplinary or Infused Model

In this model a distinct environment education unit, course or module is created by selecting, presenting and dwelling upon the relevant components of various disciplines.

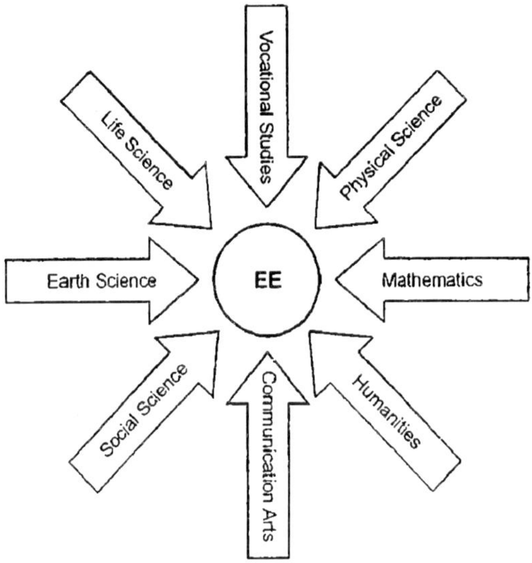

Fig. 2.2: Indisciplinary or Fused Model of Environmental Education

2. Multidisciplinary or Infusion Model

In this model, concept of Environmental Education and problem solving skills are incorporated in various disciplines wherever appropriate. No separate unit, course or module is created.

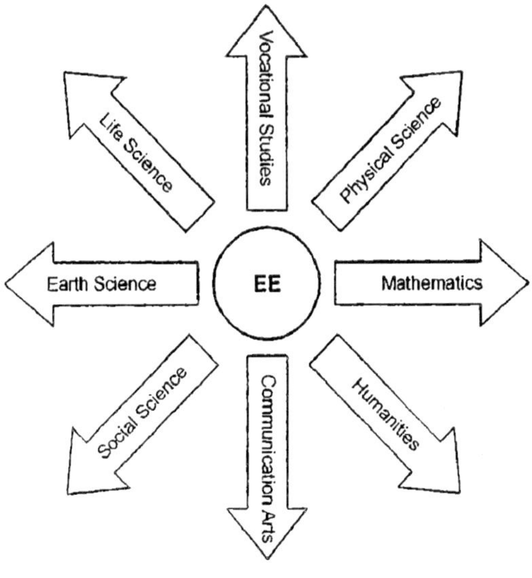

Fig. 2.3: Multidisciplinary or Infused Model of Environmental Education

Source: *UNESCO Strategies for Developing EE Curriculum*, Paris, 1986.

At the primary stage, multidisciplinary approach may be followed on account of the following factors:

1. Environmental topics can be easily handled by a single teacher with some elementary training.
2. No additional subject will be introduced.

Therefore, there is no overloading of the primary school curriculum.

At the middle and secondary stages, interdisciplinary approach should be adopted. This will be helpful in taking up environmental issues in an integrated way. At these stages, a detailed treatment is required. When related topics are introduced in different subjects, there is overlapping. Of course, it should be included as a separate unit in social sciences or sciences.

At the senior secondary stage, Environmental Education/Studies should be introduced as a separate discipline also.

CONCEPTUAL MODEL OF ENVIRONMENTAL EDUCATION CURRICULUM BASED ON THE 'GOAL LEVELS'

The model in the Figure 2.4 illustrates a conceptual scheme. How the 'scope' (Operationalized from goal level) can be integrated through grade levels (vertical organisation) and across appropriate disciplines (horizontal organisation).

The scope (or breadth) defines the extent of converge by the curriculum in terms of objectives (cognitive, affective and psychomotor) or statements of ideas or conceptual schemes. the sequence assigns these elements to grade levels based on a hierachy of concepts, skills and attitudes.

In this model the curriculum development goals are organised into four levels which are hierarchical with respect to the development of knowledge, skills and attitudes. However, they are not necessarily restricted to particular grade levels. Certain goals for level III could be used for curriculum development in the primary grades (age-group 5–8), whereas certain contents for Level II may be found desirable for higher grades with adults.

Following are brief explanations about these four levels and the associated goals:

Level I. These goals focus on *ecological* concepts. This is 'knowledge

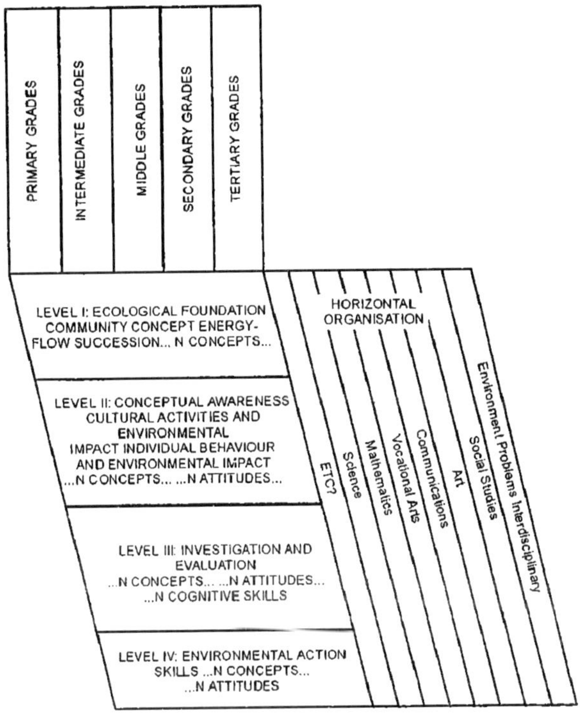

Fig. 2.4: A Conceptual Model of the Scope and Sequence of the EE Curriculum

Source: *Strategies for Developing on Environmental Education Curiculum*, UNESCO, Paris, 1980.

level'. It provides learners with that knowledge which can help them make ecologically sound environmental decisions. The details of conceptual components are to be designed by the curriculum developer.

Level II. This is also 'knowledge level' focussing on information (*conceptual awareness*) concerning many aspects of human environmental behaviour. Goals at this level assist learners to conceptualise how man's cultural activities (religious, economic, political, social, etc.) influence the environment from an ecological perspective. This level aims at to developing a conceptual awareness of how individual and collective human actions can influence the relationship between the quality of life and the quality of the environment, and of how these actions result in environmental issues which must be resolved through investigation, evaluation, values clarification, decision making and finally, citizenship action.

Level III. This level is a cognitive process or 'skill level' which focusses on those skills needed for *investigation, evaluation and values clarification of issues*.

Level IV. This level is also a 'process' or 'environmental action skills level' (*training* and *application*). It focusses on those processes and skills important for citizenship participation. This level seeks to guide the development of those skills necessary for learners to take positive environmental action for the purpose of achieving and/or maintaining a dynamic balance between the quality of life and the quality of the environment.

UNIFIED APPROACH TO THE TEACHING OF ENVIRONMENTAL EDUCATION

A unified approach to the teaching of the environmental education is a guiding principle in the field of environmental education. The content of this principle is reflected in the materials of the Tbilisi Conference and summarised in the following major provisions.

1. Environmental education is an integral part of the education process. It should be centred on practical problems and be of an interdisciplinary character.
2. Within the framework of formal education all elements of the education process should be taken into account (curricula and programmes, works of literature and textbooks, teaching aids, methods, etc.) and gradually reach interdisciplinary. Without denying the existence and individuality of each classical discipline, it is necessary to avoid an excessively analytical character in the disciplines and allow for differences connected with their methods, since these make it difficult for the students to perceive the environment as a whole. An approach based on consistent abstraction leads pupils away from proper study of the environment. In this connection the following solutions are possible; to develop educational programmes by interdisciplinary teams; and to study concrete environmental problems.
3. Environmental education should not be just one more subject to add to existing programmes, but should be incorporated into programmes intended for all learners, irrespective of their age. Environmental education should play the role of a catalyst,

or common denominator, in the renovated process of modern instruction. It is necessary to establish and uphold clear and functional ties between requirements, goals, tasks, the programme itself and evaluation methods.

4. Special preference should be given to various social groups who find themselves in less favourable conditions in many countries, for instance, illiterate people. Therefore, it is necessary to find for them ways of education by means of providing functional literacy, including aspects of the environment (at the beginning, aspects of their social, and later professional milieu).
5. Environmental education should not be a matter of 'competition' with various disciplines which are at present included in the educational plan; it should be a means for promoting the recognition by pupils of certain unity of the educational process and make it possible for them to develop the knowledge, skills and attitudes for preserving and improving their environment.
6. Certain environmental problems are not related to the sphere of direct youth experience, and even for experienced students the understanding of environmental problems demands conceptualisation, the ability to expound things on the basis of comparatively abstract symbols. The primary rule is to accord the means of education with the intellectual and physical stage of the recipient (learner) and in accord with all other important pedagogical laws, specially with the specific principles of environmental education. Secondary schools should concentrate on the ecological, social, political and economic aspects of environmental education.
7. The interdisciplinary aspect of environmental education predetermines the teacher's development of such education programmes of nationally adapted courses to ensure the necessary minimum environmental education for pupils. Regardless of regional aspects of education and forms of teaching, these programmes should include a compulsory set of topics and questions which would be gradually expounded during the study of particular disciplines, taking into account the term of study and age of the pupil.

Source: Environmental Education: Module in In-service Training of Science Teachers and Supervisors of Secondary Schools. UNESCO, Paris, 1983.

TEACHING METHODS

Content and methods of teaching environmental education were set forth in the recommendations of the Tbilisi Conference which considered:

1. that the separate disciplines which may bear on environmental issues are often taught in isolation from each other and may tend to neglect or pay insufficient attention to environmental problems;
2. that separate as well as interdisciplinary approaches both have important parts to play, depending on situations, learning groups and age levels;
3. that teaching methods for either type of approach are still in the process of development;
4. that the incorporation of environmental education into existing curricula or teaching programmes is often slow;
5. that the criteria on which to base the content of environmental education programmes and curricula are also in need of further development;
6. that historic and cultural landscapes and situations also demand special consideration.
7. that particular sections of the community, such as farmers, rural inhabitants, managers, industrial workers and others, need specially adapted environmental education programmes;
8. that in most if not all programmes and curricula, the teaching of ecological concepts plays a fundamentally important role;
9. that environmental education should preferably be oriented towards the solution of problems (problem-solving approach) and be concerned with opportunities for action (action-oriented approach)...Research relevant to these different approaches, aspects and methods is needed to provide a sound basis for the development of environmental education curricula and programmes, so the Conference recommended.
10. that educational and training institutions should have the necessary flexibility to enable them to include appropriate aspects of environmental education within existing curricula and to create new environmental curricula that meet the requirements of an interdisciplinary approach and methodology;

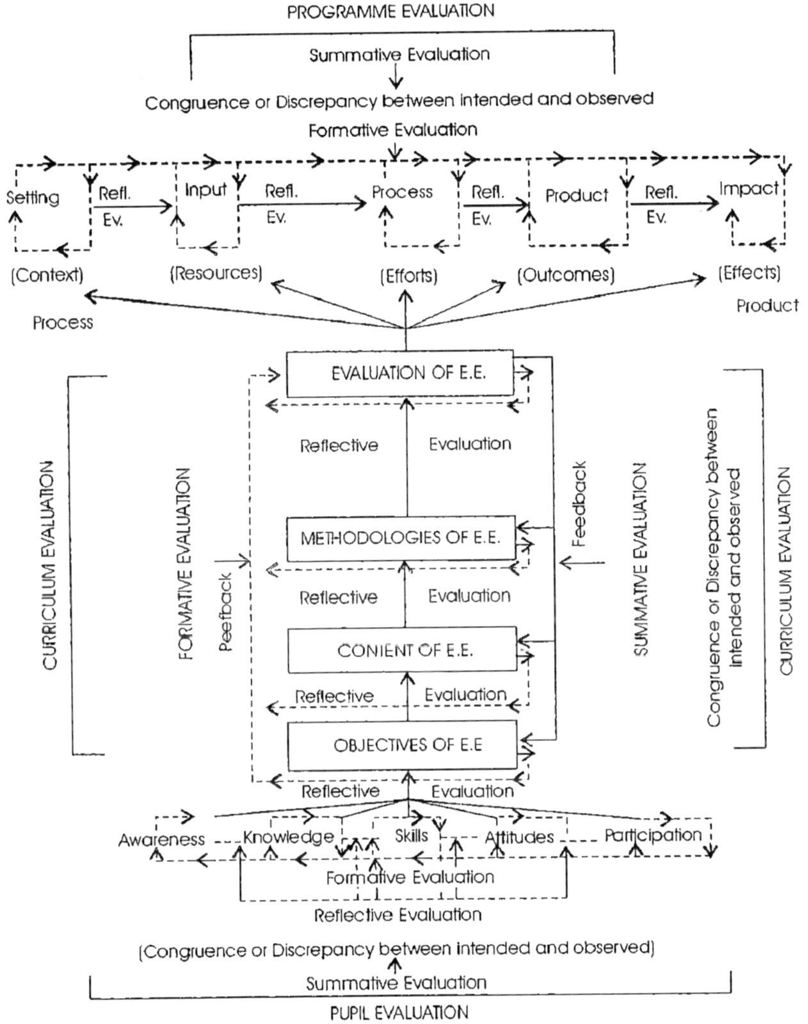

Fig. 2.5: Methodology of Environmental Education

Source: *Environmental Education at the School Level. A Lead Paper*, NCERT (1981).

11. that relevant authorities work out criteria on which to base the environmental content of the curricula to be offered to pupils and students according to individual needs and taking into account local, social, occupational and other factors;
12. that within the framework of individual systems, encouragement and support might be provided for subject disciplines to identify and give priority to their special contribution to environmental education; and for those

responsible for the planning and carrying out of programmes of general and vocational education to encourage that through interdepartmental collaboration and co-ordination, environmental aims and objectives are adequately served;

13. that they examine the potential of appropriate institutions to carry out research into the development of curricula and programmes in environmental education and encourage necessary initiatives, including institutional co-operation;
14. that responsible authorities support curriculum development as it relates to particular situations such as exist in urban areas, rural areas and areas of social, historical and cultural importance, and to the needs of particular groups such as farmers, industrial workers and parents;
15. that in all approaches full and adequate emphasis is given to the teaching of ecological concepts, to the systems of the atmosphere, lithosphere, hydrosphere and biosphere and to relevant socio-economic aspects.

Flexibility and Variety of Teaching Methods

The flexibility and variety of teaching methods of education in the environmental field depend on the contingent of students, their age and form of instruction and on the professional skills of the teacher. From this point of view, environmental subjects differ from a number of other courses in that they involve problems of immediate concern to the students. Nature conservation themes should be integrated into all lessons gradually. The main goal here is to evoke the interest of children in each nature object and foster respect and sympathy for every thing because each organism is inimitable and a link in the chain of complicated natural relationships and interrelationships.

Nature and labour are the main sources of life and development on the Earth. That is why lessons should be supplemented by the participation of pupils in various practical environment protection activities.

The flexibility and variety of teaching methods also depend to a great extent on how the teacher motivates students with the very idea of environmental protection, what conceptions and categories he or she uses and what practical material is the basis of the instruction.

Of great importance is the teacher's personal conviction of the need to teach interdisciplinary environmental issues at all levels of formal and non-formal education.

Finally, it should be emphasised that the success of environmental education largely depends on a will developed system of instruction and on consistency in the presentation of its various issues.

3

Objectives and Curriculum of Environmental Education at the School Stage

PRIMARY STAGE (CLASSES I TO V)

(a) Rationale of Introducing Environmental Studies at the Primary Stage

Keeping in view the developmental characteristics and needs of the child at primary stage (age group 6–11 years), the National Curriculum Framework for School Education (NCFSE) brought out by the NCERT in 2000 has perceived Environmental Studies as an integrated area.

In Classes I and II, the environmental concerns are to be taken care of through the curricular areas of Languages, Mathematics and Art of Healthy and Productive Living (AHPL).

Environmental studies are to be taught as an independent curricular area in Classes III to V.

The focus of this area of study should be on developing an awareness about the environment and on developing habits, attitudes and skills in the child for being a healthy and active member of the community.

The following concerns guide the approach and treatment of the curricular area:

1. Explosion of knowledge due to developments in various fields, making to-day's knowledge outdated tommorrow.
2. Changes in ways and quality of life due to advancements in science and technology.
3. Changes in social set-up due to replacement of joint family system by nuclear families.

(b) General Objectives

The objectives of Environmental Studies at Primary Stage are to help the child to be:

- *physically, emotionally, socially and mentally* healthy;
- able to *function effectively* as a member of the social groups (family, community) she/he belongs to;
- able to *develop skills, attitudes and values* for improving the quality of life of self and that of the community;
- able to *appreciate the need* to live in harmony with nature.

(c) Expected learning Outcomes (ELO)

I. Learning to Know

The child will:

- *develop an understanding* of basic structure and functions of various parts of human body and the need to take care of these parts;
- *develop an understanding* of social, cultural, natural and man-made environment and their interrelationships;
- *develop awareness and understanding* about her/his personal well-being, belongings and surroundings and ways to keep them clean;
- *demonstrate an understanding* for conservation of natural resources and protection of the environment and also take action for protecting it and proper utilisation of resources;
- *demonstrate an understanding* of distance in space and time and the relationship between them.

II. Learning to Do

The child will:

- *develop competencies* and skills for *lifelong learning (for quality of life)*, i.e., skills of observation, reporting, collecting information, discrimination, classification, experimentation, making predictions and estimations, drawing inferences, etc;
- *interpret and report observations in a variety of ways*—oral, written, pictorial (graphs, charts, tables);

- *practice healthy habits* such as cleanliness, discipline, punctuality, proper care of belongings, etc;
- *develop healthy attitude* towards dignity of labour and prepare adequately to face life;
- *develop skills of reading* a map and locating places in the map;
- *develop skills of using* the globe;
- *develop skills of using* standard and non-standard units of measurement;
- *plan and carryout* simple and safe experiments/activities on her/ his own/under the guidance of the teacher.

III. Learning to Live Together

The child will:

- *develop social skills and values*, such as sharing, caring/helping others (including differently abled children) tolerance, team-spirit, cooperation, working together for common good, waiting for ones turn, etc;
- *learn to live in harmony* with the environment and people of different communities and having different faiths;
- *recognise and appreciate the contributions made by people* in the past and in the present for the well-being of the community;
- *respect rules* made for the benefit of the community and follow them.

IV. Learning to Be

The child will:

- *understand and play her/his role* as an individual in home, at school, and the community (neighbourhood);
- *express herself/himself freely* in creative activities;
- acquire habits of self-learning through creative/productive activities;
- develop *ability to ask simple questions* relating to natural and social environment;
- *practice some positive values* specific to her/his own context, e.g. truthfulness, honesty, brotherhood, patriotism, etc;
- *appreciate beauty in the environment* and show a sense of aesthetic appreciation through expression in varied forms of art;
- *appreciate* culture and traditions and take pride in being an Indian;

- *show and promote respect and concern* for others and for the environment;
- *develop abilities to process information* and take independent decisions in simple situations in day-to-day life;
- *develop scientific temper.*

COURSE CONTENT, TEACHING-LEARNING MATERIAL AND TEACHING-LEARNING STRATEGIES

Course Content for Classes I and II

Although Environmental Studies is not an independent curricular area in Classes I and II, it was felt that integration of its relevant expected learning outcomes in language and mathematics must be ensured. This would provide the foundation for initiating Environmental Studies as an area of study from Class III onwards.

(1) My Body
(2) My Needs
(3) My Family and My Home
(4) My Neighbourhood
(5) Transport and Communication
(6) Natural Environment.

Classes III to V

Theme: Me and My Surroundings

1. My Body
2. My Needs:
   (i) Food-water, Air
   (ii) Shelter
   (iii) Clothing
   (iv) Health and Hygiene
   (v) Recreation
   (vi) Community Service
3. My surroundings
   (i) Natural Phenomena and Resources
   (ii) Transport and Communication.

Teaching-learning Material

Considering the nature of the curricular area, the best materials are the objects in the environment and real life day-to-day situations.

For classroom interaction a wider range of materials would be required, which may comprise the following:

- Textbook-cum-Activity Book (one for each class) in the form of units based on sub-themes listed in the course content in the curriculum.
- Locally available concrete material, and aids like charts, pictures, maps, globe, models, apparatus for conducting experiments, etc.
- Different media such as library books, magazines, newspapers, radio and television and pre-recorded programmes.

Teaching-learning Strategies

Keeping in view the varied needs of curricular area and those of the children, the teacher is expected to adopt a variety of teaching-learning strategies. These can range from practical experiences in real life situations to creating similar situations (simulation) through the use of concrete or audio/visual materials. Thus, the teacher can adopt any of the following strategies or their combination as per the demands of the situation:

- Environmental visits
- Guided simple experiments
- Projects
- Individual/group activities
- Quiz/Puzzles/games
- Role-play/drama
- Teacher-guided classroom activities.

ENVIRONMENTAL EDUCATION IN CLASSES VI TO VIII

Environmental Education/Studies form part of Social Sciences and Science and Technology.

Objectives

1. develop an understanding of natural, human resources and their potentialities for a better to-morrow;
2. acquire a positive attitude towards conservation and preservation of environment, its resources and heritage;

3. create an awareness of the immediate environment and the need for its protection;
4. acquaint children with the technology that abounds in their immediate surroundings.

I. Course Structure of Environment Studies and Learning Outcomes of the Teaching of Social Sciences

Unit I: The Earth—Our Habitat

Content Outline	*Learning Outcomes*
	This Unit will enable the learners to:
• Four realms of the earth: lithosphere, hydrosphere, atmosphere and biosphere.	• explain interrelationship of the realms of the earth;
• Major relief features of the earth: continents and oceans.	• understand major landforms of the earth;
• India in the world: physiographic divisions of India—mountains, plateaus and plains; climate; natural vegetation and wild life, need for their conservation.	• comprehend broad physiographic divisions of India;
Project/Activity	• describe the influence of land, climate, vegetation and wildlife on human life;
• Make a chart showing common trees in the surrounding and classify them on the basis of various uses such as fruits, flowers, fibres and others. • Show the major wildlife sanctuaries of your region on a political map of India. • Arrange for a trip to a Wildlife Sanctuary or Zoo. *Note*: *Any two activities to be taken.*	• appreciate the need for conserving natural vegetation and wildlife.

Class VII

Unit II: Our Environment

• Environment in its totality: natural and human environment.	This Unit will enable the learners to:
• Natural Environment: land—interior of the earth, rocks and minerals; earth movements and major land forms.	• understand the environment in its totality including various components both natural and human;

(Contd.)

Content Outline	*Learning Outcomes*
• Air—composition, structure of the atmosphere, elements of weather and climate—temperature, pressure, moisture and wind.	• explain the components of natural environment;
• Water—fresh and saline, distribution of major water bodies, ocean waters and their circulation.	• appreciate the interdependence of these components and their importance in our life;
• Natural vegetation and wild life.	• appreciate and develop sensitivity towards environment;
• Human Environment: settlement, transport and communication.	• explain the relationship between natural environment and human habitation;
• Human—Environment Interaction: Case Studies—life in desert regions—Sahara and Ladakh; life in tropical and sub-tropical regions—Amazon and Ganga-Brahmaputra; life in temperate regions—Prairies and the Veldt.	• be familiar with the new developments making today's world a global society;
• Write observations about local cultural environment, house types, settlement, transport, communication and vegetation.	• understand the complex inter-relationship of human and natural environment;
• Collect stories/find out about the changes that took place in their areas (identify how things/surroundings change overnight and why).	• compare life in one's own surrounding with life of other environmental settings;
• Gather more information on areas similar to the case studies done in the chapter and see how are they different from ours.	• appreciate the cultural differences existing in the world which is an outcome of interaction, between human beings and their environment;
Note: Any one activity to be taken	

Unit III: India—Land and the people

• *India*: Location, Relief, Structure, Major Physiographic Units, Rocks and Minerals, Soils, their Distribution, Impact on life.	This UNIT will enable the learners to:
• *Climate*: Factors Influencing the Climate; Monsoon—Its Characteristics, Rainfall and Temperature Distribution; Seasons; Climate and Human Life.	• understand the major landform features and the underlying geological structure; their association with various rocks and minerals as well as nature of soil types;

(Contd.)

(*Contd.*)

Content Outline	Learning Outcomes
• *Drainage*: Major Rivers and Tributaries, Lakes and Seas, Role of Rivers in the Economy, Pollution of Rivers, Measures to Control River Pollution. • *Natural Vegetation*: Vegetation Types, Distribution as well as Altitudinal Variation. Need for Conservation and Various Measures.	• identify the various factors influencing the climate and explain the climatic variation of our country and its impact on the life of the people; • explain the importance and unifying role of monsoons;
• *Wildlife*: Major species, their distribution. Need for Conservation and Various Measures.	• describe the river systems of the country and explain the role of rivers in the evolution of human society;
• *Population*: Size, Distribution, Age-Sex Composition, Population Change—Migration as a Determinant of Population Change, Literacy, Health Occupational Structure, and National Population Policy: Adolescents as Under-Served Population Group with Special Needs.	• find out the nature of diverse flora and fauna as well as their distribution;
Project/Activity	• develop concern about the need to protect the bio-diversity of our country • analyse the uneven nature of population distribution and show concern about the large size of our population;
Survey: • Major landform features of the locality and its influence on social features i.e., transport-communication and settlement. *Activity is to be accompanied by a brief report.*	• discuss the various occupations of people and explain various factors of population change. • explain various dimensions of national population policy and understand the needs of adolescents as under-served group.
Posters: • River Pollution • Rainfall Harvesting • Depletion of Forests and Global Warming/Soil Erosion. *Note:* One activity is to be undertaken	

II. Course Content of Environmental Education Under Science and Technology

Objectives

1. Create an awareness of the immediate environment and a need for its protection.

2. Acquaint the children with the technology that abounds their immediate surroundings.

Course Structure

Class VI

Unit 1: Our Earth. This Includes

- Factors essential for life on earth
- Structure of earth—crust, mantle and core
- Atmosphere, oceans, water and soil
- Earth and the solar system.
- Uniqueness of the planet earth.

Unit 2: Our Environment—This Includes

- Physical and biological environment
- Biotic and abiotic components
- Biotic components—plants and animals
- Abiotic components—light, temperature, air, water and soil
- Interaction between abiotic and biotic components
- Socio-cultural environment.

Class VII

Unit 1: Life on Earth

- Role of man in the conservation, maintenance and judious use of resources of the earth with reference to forest, soils, minerals, water and air.

Unit 2: Water

- Water Pollution—cases and prevention.

Unit 3

Noise—Class VIII

1. Soil pollution and erosion and their prevention
2. Air pollution—causes and prevention

3. Green house effect; acid rain.

COURSE CONTENT AND OBJECTIVES OF ENVIRONMENT EDUCATION IN SOCIAL SCIENCES (CLASSES IX, X)

Objectives

1. To deepen the knowledge and understanding of India's environment in its totality, its interactive processes and effects on the future quality of people's lives.
2. To promote an understanding of the issues and challenges of contemporary India—environmental aspects as economic and social part of the developmental process.
3. To develop concern about the need and to protect the bio-diversity of our population.
4. To develop concern about the protection of flora and fauna.
5. To understand the need for conservation of resources.

Class IX

1. Climate and human life
2. Measures to control river pollution
3. *Wildlife*: major species, their distribution, need for conservation and various measures
4. Population.

Class X

Unit 4:

1. Degradation and conservation of natural resources
2. Forest and wildlife, conservation and protection of forests and wildlife
3. Need for conservation of water resources and checking pollution
4. Industrial pollution and degradation of environment. Measures to control degradation

Course content and objectives of Environmental Education in Science and Technology (Classes IX and X).

Objectives

1. develop an understanding of the various processes of environment and concerns for its conservation and preservation
2. develop rich and satisfying view of the universe.

Course Content of Environmental Education

Class IX

Unit 5: Environment

1. Habitat and adaptation
2. Eco-system.

Class X

Unit 5: Environment

1. Causes, prevention and control of soil erosion, pollution of air, water and etc.
2. Ecological balance
3. Environment and development
4. Environmental Laws.

COURSE CONTENT OF ENVIRONMENTAL EDUCATION AT THE HIGHER SECONDARY STAGE (CLASSES XI AND XII)

Geography

Class XI. Life on the Earth. Wildlife. Soil conservation. Natural Hazards.

Class XII. Resources and Sustainable Development. Environmental Pollution.

Economics

Class XI.

Population: Environment.

OBJECTIVES OF ENVIRONMENTAL EDUCATION AT VARIOUS LEVELS OF SCHOOL STAGE SUGGESTED BY SAVITA SINHA AND KUSUM PREMI

Savita Sinha and Kusum Premi in *Environmental Education*, NIEPA/ UNESCO, 1988 suggest the following guidelines for the development of objectives of EE at the primary and secondary levels:

1. There should be a continuity between the objectives developed for the primary level and those developed for the secondary level.
2. The achievement of primary level objectives should be considered as pre-requisite to the achievements of the secondary level objectives.

3. The objectives should be to develop cognitive as also affective domains of learning.
4. Curricular materials developed should focus on the development of desired knowledge, skills and attitudes.

Objectives of Environmental Education at the Primary Level

1. To make the child aware of his environment in a very simple manner and his place in it.
2. To arouse interest in the people around him and develop understanding of the environment.
3. To develop skills for learning about the environment i.e., observation, collection and classification.
4. To develop willingness to work individually and in groups to maintain and preserve the environment.
5. To foster development of positive attitude in pupils towards their environment.

Objectives of Environmental Education at the Secondary Level

1. To broaden pupils' concept of environment and man's place in it.
2. To stimulate reading for upgrading factual knowledge concerning short as well as long-term effects of misuse and abuse of the environment.
3. To reinforce attitudes favourable to continued involvement in environment education and develop social responsibility towards improving his/her environment.
4. To equip pupils to live satisfactorily in the society by way of meaningful contribution through increased knowledge of the environment.
5. To reinforce and further develop positive attitudes towards environment.
6. To develop skills to collect and classify data, compare and contrast, identify and solve problems.
7. To enhance perception which will enable students to appraise and propose measures for improvement of environment.

INSTRUCTIONAL OBJECTIVES OF ENVIRONMENTAL STUDIES/ EDUCATION AT THE PRIMARY STAGE SUGGESTED BY DR. S.K. MITRA

Prof. Shiv K. Mitra, a former Director of NCERT in his preface to *An Approach to Education in Environment Studies at the Primary Stage*

(1980) has very rightly observed, "It is accepted on all hands that immediate environment lays the most important foundation of education in the formative years. The recent educational literature is also increasingly emphasising the exploitation of this vital source for realising the cherished goal of a harmonious and optimal pupil growth."

A publication of the NCERT entitled *Instructional Objectives of School Subjects* (1989) has given the following instructional objectives of Environmental Studies at the primary stage. For all purposes, these objectives may be considered as objectives of environmental education also at the primary stage.

Objectives and Specifications of Environmental Studies (Environmental Education) for Classes I–V

1. *Observation*. To develop the ability to implore the world around them (Learners) with specific purpose, to recognise and identify objects so as to find relationships between new and observed facts using all their senses. (This process does inculcate a sense of personal satisfaction in knowing and exploring the environment through direct experience.)

Specifications of the Objectives

The pupil

1.1 recognises the properties of objects and phenomena using the senses of sight, sound, taste, smell and touch;

1.2 recalls the properties of objects from previous experiences;

1.3 identifies objects, events and changes occurring in the environment;

1.4 distinguishes objects on the basis of their properties, and develops a habit of noting minute differences in the characteristics of objects and phenomena;

1.5 voluntarily seeks new information about the physical and social environment;

1.6 develops curiosity to see now objects of the environment.

2. *Classification*. To develop the ability to discriminate order, arrange, give sequence, observe events using given or chosen criteria in order to compare phenomenon. (The process develops an awareness of the diversity of systems and the importance of ordering and interpreting phenomena).

Specifications of the Objective

The pupil

2.1 describes differences between objects and phenomena on the basis of given or chosen criteria;
2.2 distinguishes between objects and phenomena on the basis of similarity and differences;
2.3 orders objects on the basis of one or more criteria;
2.4 identifies and names properties which could serve as the basis for possible classifications;
2.5 appreciates that there are several different ways of grouping objects and events.

3. *Counting and Measurement.* To develop the ability to identify the purpose of measurement, to select which type of measurement would serve the purpose and how the measurement is to be taken and recorded in order to make inferences about relationships between variables in the environment.

Specifications of the Objective

The pupil

3.1 identifies sets and their members;
3.2 compares areas and masses of different shapes and sizes;
3.3 demonstrates measurement of length, area, time, temperature and volume using relevant instruments;
3.4 orders numbers;
3.5 determines number relationships;
3.6 distinguishes differences between estimation and measurement of objects and phenomena;
3.7 Selects situations when measurement and estimation are to be used for determining length, weight, area, distance, size, etc;
3.8 compares, measures and makes inferences about the variables;
3.9 designs tables for recording data;
3.10 prefers to accurate in measurement;
3.11 appreciates the need to measure for interpreting relationships between phenomena.

4. *Use of Space-time Relationship.* To develop the ability to identify the relationships in the social physical environment between

movement of time and the changes that occur in social and physical processes.

Specifications of the Objective

The pupil

4.1 recognises specified objects in relation to other objects;
4.2 identifies direction and movement of objects in space;
4.3 interprets trends and the changes in environmental phenomena;
4.4 compares changes in the spatial position and relationships between physical and social phenomena over time;
4.5 develops tentative generalisations to explain changes in social and physical phenomena over space and in time;
4.6 appreciates the dynamic nature of natural and social systems and develops awareness of the diversity and constant change of social and physical processes.

5. *Experimentation and Investigation.* To develop the ability to pose questions which require investigation, to suggest and use procedures, to collect, organise and interpret data, to derive generalisations. (Considering the stage of development of the child, the experiments would range from simple to complex.)

Specification of the Objective

The pupil

5.1 poses questions and identifies problems which are likely to be answered by investigation and experimentation;
5.2 suggests possible or tentative conclusions;
5.3 establishes possible relationships between variables;
5.4 constructs and/or assembles relevant apparatus for experimentation;
5.5 prepares appropriate tools for investigation;
5.6 conducts experiments and investigations systematically;
5.7 shows perseverance in undertaking experiments and investigations;
5.8 skillfully manipulates instruments;
5.9 obeys safety regulations;
5.10 voluntarily undertakes care and maintenance of tools, materials and living things;
5.11 Practises honesty in reporting results.

6. *Analysis and Interpretation.* To develop the ability to identify the relationships between variables to infer cause and effect relationships and to deduce conclusions derived by investigation and experimentation.

Specifications of the Objective

The Pupil

6.1 organises data efficiently;
6.2 recognises central themes/issues and assumptions;
6.3 compares trends and patterns of observed phenomenon;
6.4 infers relationships between different phenomena;
6.5 establishes relationships between variables;
6.6 suspends judgments till adequate data is available;
6.7 forms a habit of systematic enquiry.

7. *Generalisation and Prediction.* To develop the ability to formulate generalisations, draw conclusions, verify facts and predict consequences on the basis of analysis and interpretation. (The appreciation of using enquiry, to form hypotheses and critical judgment of evidences is an outcome of this process.)

Specifications of the Objective

The pupil

7.1 deduces relationships between variables;
7.2 verifies conclusions with further evidence;
7.3 extrapolates trends, implications, assumptions based on obtained data and previous knowledge;
7.4 derives principles on the basis of relationships between variables;
7.5 appreciates the need to revise opinions on the basis of newly available facts;
7.6 supports ideas and arguments with sound and logical arguments.

8. *Communication.* To develop the ability to express through writing, speech and action, relevant observations, conclusions and arguments. (The requisite skills to understand and use information through the development of the skills to read, listen, see and locate information effectively is an expected outcome of this process.)

4

Environmental Pollution: Types, Causes and Remedies

MEANING OF ENVIRONMENTAL POLLUTION AND POLLUTANTS

Environmental pollution is defined as an undesirable change in our surroundings, wholly or partially, in the physical, chemical or biological characteristics of air, water or land. The change may affect man directly, affect the desirable plants and animals and/or affect our raw material resources.

Pollution may also be defined as undesirable and excessive addition of substances in air, water or land which adversely alter the natural quality of our environment.

Pollution could be natural or by undesirable activities of man.

Pollutant: The agent that pollutes the environment is termed as pollutant. A pollutant is a substance present in the environment in concentrations that are harmful to the environment and to the living beings.

A pollutant can also be defined as a substance present in the *wrong amount*, at the *wrong place* and at the wrong time.

For example, nitrogen and phosphorus are essential nutrients for plants and are extensively used in agriculture, but they can cause pollution in lakes when found in excess and cause death of animals in water.

Classification of Pollutants

Depending on whether the pollutants can be broken down into simpler and harmless products or not, they can be broadly classified into following two types:

1. Biodegradable pollutants.
2. Non-biodegradable pollutants.

Types of Pollutants

Biodegradable pollutants	**Non-biodegradable pollutants**
• Pollutants are biodegradable i.e. can be broken down by the activity of microorganisms and enter the biogeochemical cycles.	• Pollutants are non-biodegradable i.e. cannot be broken down to simpler and harmless products. They cannot enter biogeochemical cycles.
• Act as pollutants only when present in large quantity and not degraded (broken down) at the right time.	• These pollutants may occur in solid, liquid or gaseous state.
	• They may enter into the food chain and harm the organism.
Examples: Domestic waste products, urine and faecal matter, sewage, agricultural residue, paper, wood and cloth.	*Example*: Insecticides, pesticides, DDT, mercury, lead, arsenic, aluminium, plastics, radioactive wastes etc.

Fig 4.1: Biodegradable Pollutants

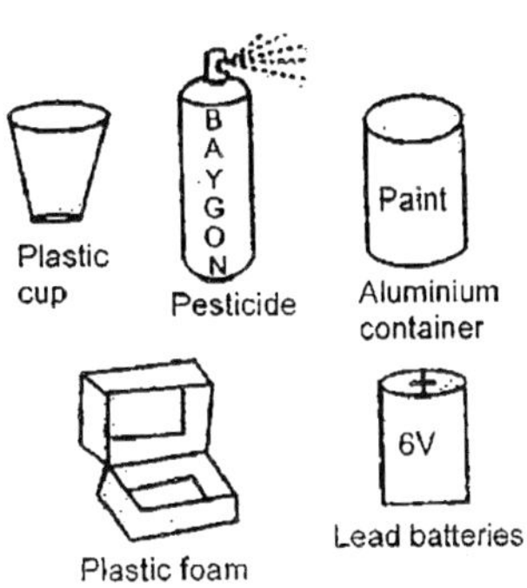

Fig. 4.2: Non-biodegradable Pollutants

TYPES OF POLLUTION

Pollutions can be classified by various ways. On the basis of the components of environment that is polluted, pollution can be of three types. These are:

1. Air pollution
2. Water pollution
3. Soil pollution (Land pollution).

NATURAL AND ARTIFICIAL SOURCES OF POLLUTION

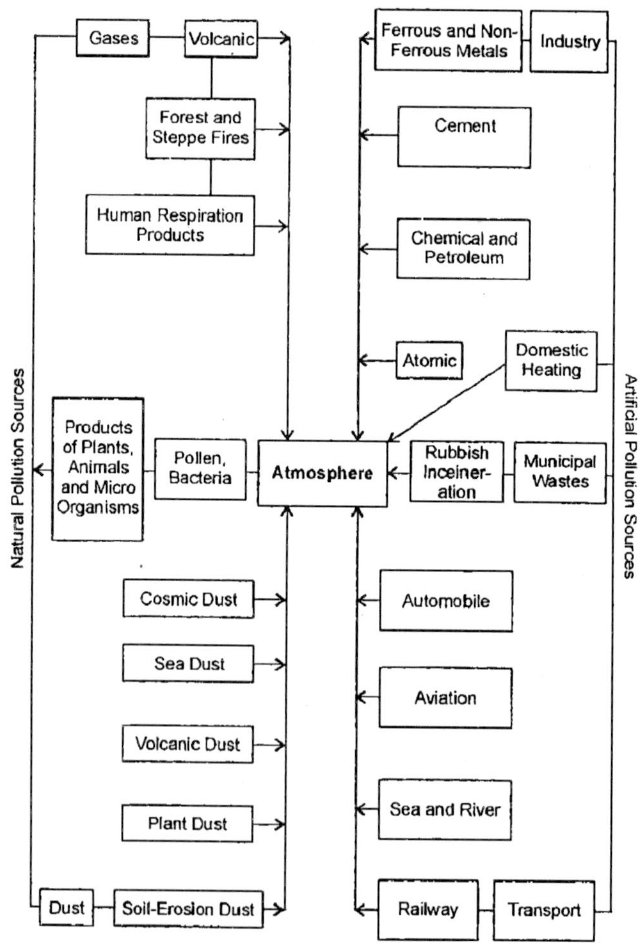

Fig. 4.3: Main Sources of Atmospheric Pollution

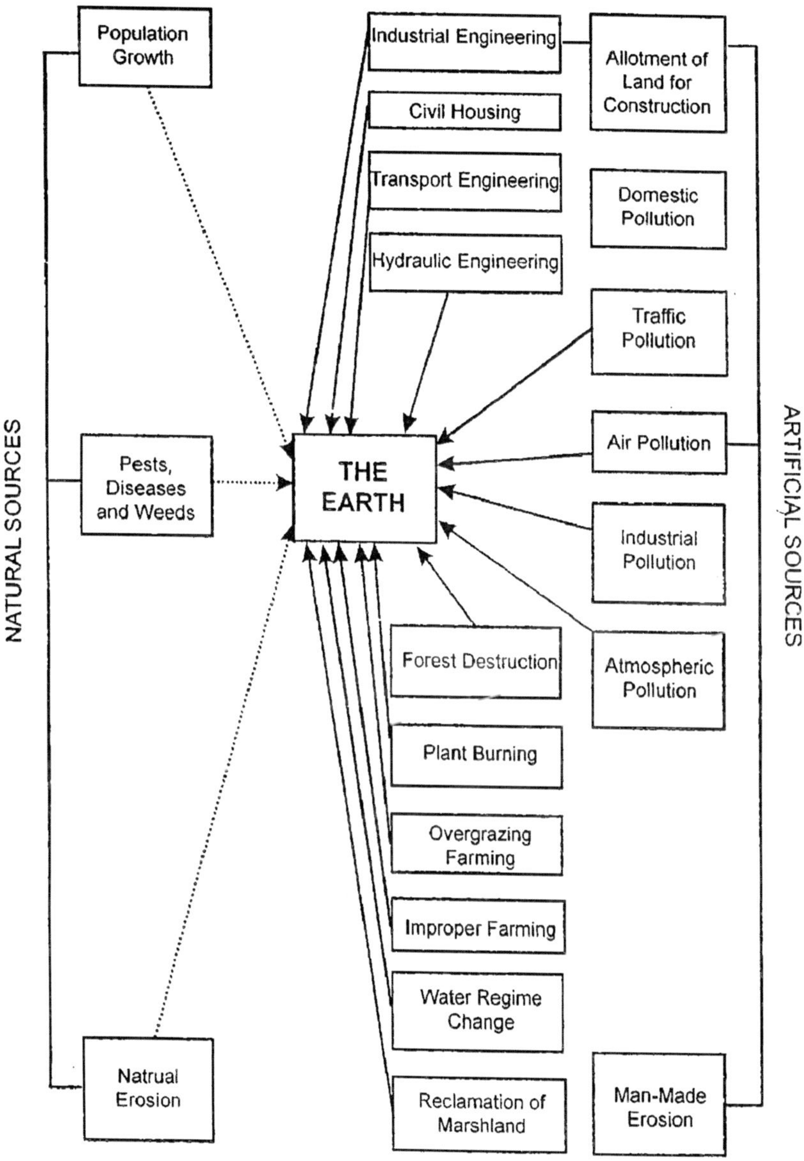

Fig. 4.4: Basic Factors Affecting Landuse and Environmental Pollution

Sources for Fig. 4.3 and 4.4 Living in the Environment UNESCO/UNEP 1985.

CAUSES OF POLLUTION

Pollution is caused when a change in physical, chemical, or biological conditions in the environment harmfully affect the quality of human life, including effects on other animals and plants, industries, and cultural and aesthetic assets. Though pollution is generally attributed to material substances (gases and particulate matter from smokestacks, chemicals in water or solid wastes, paper, glass, used automobiles), pollution may also be non-material, such as an excess of noise and light. Pollution in all its forms is a more serious problem in the heavily industrialised areas of the world than it is in predominantly agricultural regions.

Even before man, nature put great quantities of material into the environment and still does (volcanoes, dust storms). Solid material in air, such as salt particles or dust, are essential as the nuclei for raindrops. Yet, when cities add massively to the amount of these nuclei, the excess may diminish rainfall because the drops that form are too small to fall as rain. Because of the multiple uses of air, water, and land, the tolerable amount or level of pollution varies.

Pollution usually occurs where people and their activities are concentrated. Generally, if all pollutants were distributed equally over the Earth, they would not exceed tolerable limits. Because of his tendency to congregate in huge cities, man himself may be considered a pollutant or major cause of inasmuch as an excess of people in one place is often the cause of deteriorating human conditions.

Causes of different types of pollution are discussed separately.

Pollution Control

Pollution control consists of the legal, institutional, scientific, and technological arrangements established to avoid or mitigate such excesses in the environment. It can be accomplished by containing pollutants at the source, by devising new technologies of manufacture that eliminate or reduce pollutants, and by reusing (recycling) materials and commodities through reprocessing and resource recovery.

AIR POLLUTION: MEANING, CAUSES, SOURCES, EFFECTS, PREVENTION AND CONTROL

Meaning of Air Pollution

Air pollution can be defined as the occurrence or release of any foreign material or gas into the atmosphere which may be harmful to man, vegetation, animals or buildings.

Air is a mixture of gases like oxygen, carbon dioxide and nitrogen. These gases are present in a particular ratio which is healthy for survival. When the concentration and ratio of these gases changes or solid particles increase, the air is said to be polluted.

Types of Air Pollutants

On the basis of the state the pollutants are emitted; they can be broadly grouped into two categories:

(i) Gaseous pollutants
(ii) Particulate pollutants.

Air Pollutants

Gaseous pollution	**Particulate pollutants**
• Substances that remain in the gaseous state in atmosphere • These are vapours of certain compounds with boiling points below 200°C.	• Substances that remain in the solid or liquid state in atmosphere • These are in the form of large particles like sand that settle down rapidly or like dust that remains suspended for a long time. Some elements like smoke do not settle at all.
Example: CO_2, SO_2, SO_3 Nitrogen Oxides (NO_2, NO_3)	*Examples*: Aerosole, smokes, fumes, particles of carbon and various metals.

Sources or Causes of Air Pollution

On the basis of the source, the air pollutants are given out; air pollution can be broadly put into two categories.

(i) Natural source
(ii) Man-made source.

There can be a number of natural or man-made sources by which air gets polluted. Some of these are given in the Table 4.1.

Table 4.1: Sources of Air Pollution and the Main Pollutants Emitted by Them

Kind of air pollution	*Source of air pollution*	*Main pollutant*
Natural pollution	• Forest Fires	CO_2, CO, Hydrocarbons
	• Volcanic eruptions	Smoke, ash, sulphurous gases, harmful dust.
	• Dust storm	Dust particles
	• Natural air pollutants	Pollens, spores, micro-organisms etc.
Man-made pollution	• Burning of fossil fuels like coal and petroleum	CO, CO_2, smoke, hydrocarbons.
	• Thermal power plants, automobile industries.	CO_2, CO, Oxides of nitrogen (NO_2, NO_3, etc).
	• Atomic energy plants	Increase in radioactivity
	• Mining activity	Addition of particulate matter to air.
	• Agricultural activities (use of fertilisers and pesticides)	Insecticides, pesticides in air.
	• Cutting of trees and deforestation	Increased amount of CO_2 in the atmosphere. This leads to global warming as a result of green house effect.
	• Use of CFCs (Chlorofluorocarbons)	Depletion of ozone (O_2) layer. Exposure to highly dangerous ultra-violet (UV) rays of sun.

Oxygen Required During Combustion

for one ton oil	10,300 m^3
for one ton coal	1,15,000 m^3
for one ton cooking gas	15,600 m^3

The more oxygen we use the less of it is available for respiration.

Harmful Effects of Air Pollution

1. *On Respiratory System.* The air pollution causes various respiratory disorders in living organisms. Organisms may suffer from bronchitis, asthma, lung cancer and pneumonia etc. Due to high air pollution in Delhi, one out of every four children suffers from asthma or bronchitis.
2. *Effect of Carbon Monoxide (CO).* Carbon monoxide is a colourless, odourless and a highly toxic gas given out by motor vehicles, charcoal stoves, cigarette smoke, gas heaters etc. It affects the central nervous system. Inhaling of CO in

large quantities is fatal. CO has 200 times more affinity to combine with haemoglobin than oxygen. It diffuses into blood stream, combines with haemoglobin and forms an irreversible compound called carboxy haemoglobin. It is poisonous, causes suffocation and in extreme cases leads to death.

3. *Depletion of Ozone Layer due to CFCs.* Chlorofluorocarbons (CFCs) are used as coolants in *refrigerators*, as propellant gases in *spray cans* containing anything from deodorants to insecticides (aerosol sprayers), and used in *fire extinguishers* etc.

   (CFCs) *damage the protective ozone layer present around the earth. Ozone acts as a protective shield against dangerous ultra violet rays of sun. Due to depletion of ozone layer caused by CFCs, Ultra Violet (UV) radiations reach the earth's surface.)*

   UV radiations cause skin cancer, weaken the immune system and cause damage to eyes (cataract of eye). UV rays also kill and damage a number of beneficial forms of life, bringing ecological disturbances.

4. *Acid Rain.* The oxides of sulphur (SO_2-sulphur dioxide, SO_3-sulphur trioxide) and oxides of nitrogen (NO-nitrous oxide, NO_2 nitrogen dioxide) dissolve in rain water and form a dilute solution of sulphuric acid and nitric acid respectively. The rain carrying these acids are called acid rain.
   - Acid rain causes severe damage to monuments, buildings and statues. The acids in rain cause corrosion of the marble or brick surface. *Many historical monuments like Taj are being damaged by acid rain. For this reason only, the industrial units near the monuments are being shifted.*
   - Acid rain makes the soil acidic. This causes gradual degradation of soil and decline in forest and crop productivity.
   - Acid rain causes irritation of eyes in humans.
   - Acid rain is poisonous to plant life, fishes and aquatic animals.

(Separately discussed in detail)

5. *Increase in Earth's Temperature due to Increased Concentration of CO_2 in Atmosphere.* CO_2 and methane absorb some of the heat radiated from earth and reflect it back towards the earth's surface. This is known as *greenhouse effect* and it helps in

keeping the earth warm enough for life to flourish. The gases CO_2 and methane are known as greenhouse gases. The greenhouse gases are released due to burning of fossil fuel (coal and petroleum), agricultural activity and deforestation.

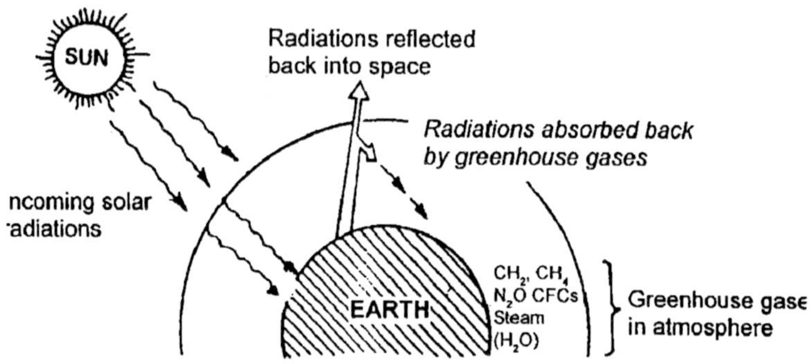

Fig: 4.5: Greenhouse Effect

- Increased burning of fossil fuel and deforestation has led to tremendous release of CO_2 in the atmosphere. Its concentration is now 25 per cent higher than pre-industrial times and is rising every year. This is leading to *increase in the earth's temperature between 2°-5°C* and this may lead to a number of consequences like—
  (i) Shifts in temperature and rainfall and variations in weather on earth (see also next chapter)
  (ii) Rise in sea-level
  (iii) Melting of ice-caps and glaciers.
  (iv) Floods and submergence of low-lying land.
  (v) Above all changes in eco-systems and socio-economic consequences.

6. *Effects of Metals.* Metal compounds released by vehicular traffic, cause a number of kidney, liver, circulatory and nervous disorders.

   Lead compounds which are discharged from the exhaust pipes of automobiles are highly toxic. They are released during the combustion of petroleum. Lead compounds when inhaled, get absorbed and cause slow poisoning as they *hamper in haemoglobin formation.* They may cause anaemia, brain damage, deterious effect on children's intelligence, convulsions and death.

7. *Effect of Pesticides.* Pesticides like DDT (Dichlorodiphenyl-trichloroethane) are highly toxic for the body.
   - These pesticides enter our body through the food chain. They get accumulated (bio magnification) at every step in food chain and reach a very high concentration in man. They cause kidney disorders and seriously damage brain and circulatory system.
   - Pesticides include insecticides, fungicides, herbicides etc. Many of these damage the nervous system severely and can be fatal also.

Occupational Hazards

Occupational hazards mean the diseases related to one's occupation. People in certain occupations are constantly exposed to certain chemicals. They inhale these chemicals from air. Over a period of time, harmful effects of these chemicals become evident on the body.

Table 4.2: Diseases Related to Occupational Hazards

Name of disease	*Agent that causes disease*	*Occupation most affected*	*Symptoms of disease*
Silicosis (Silico-tuberculosis)	Inhalation of free silica or silicon dioxide (SiO_2).	Mining, working in industries related to pottery, ceramic, glass, building, construction work etc.	• Chronic cough • Pain in the chest • Difficulty in breathing
Asbestosis	Inhaling of *asbestos*	Industries related to making of asbestos sheets (used in making ceilings)	Causes cancer. *Asbestos is a cancer causing agent.*
Byssinosis	Inhalation of *cotton fibres* over a long period of time	Textile or cloth making industries, carpet weaving industries.	• Chronic cough and asthma • Chronic bronchitis • Affects lungs severely
Pneumoconiosis	Inhalation of *coal dust*	Working in coal mining industry	• Severe lungs problems • Chronic cough difficulty in

Effects of Air Pollution on Humans

(i) SO_2 gets into soft tissues and produces drying of the mouth, scratchy throat and irritation of eyes. The formation of sulphuric acid damages the tissues.

(ii) CO diffuses into the blood stream and combines with haemoglobin to form an irreversible compound and hence stops the oxygen transport which could be fatal.

(iii) NO_x being comparative insoluble at high concentrations affects the functioning of lungs as it causes accumulation of water in air spaces.

(iv) Pollutants like hydrocarbons are carcinogenic.

(v) The air pollutants like spores, or cells of fungi, pollen grains, bacteria, fur and hair cause allergic reactions, bronchial asthma and other infections. Cotton dust, an important pollutant in Ahmedabad, Surat and other textile area causes bronchitis and asthma.

(vi) The polluted air causes various respiratory disorders. In heavily polluted areas like Delhi, one out of every 4 children suffers from asthma or bronchitis.

Effects of Air Pollution on Vegetation

(i) SO_2 damages crops and other plants.

(ii) Fluorides damage the leaf tissue.

(iii) Photochemical smog beaches and blazes the important leafy plants.

(iv) Hydrocarbons like ethylene cause premature leaf fall, flower bud shedding, curling of petals and discolouration of sepals.

(v) Certain epiphytic lichens (*Paramolia usnea, Cladonea*), and bryophytes (mosses) are reliable indicators of air pollution and can often be ranked in a sensitivity scale to estimate changing levels of atmospheric pollution, especially the content of SO_2. The presence or absence of certain common but sensitive species of epiphytic lichens and mosses in a given locality and the pattern of their distribution can be related to the extent of pollution in that area over a certain period of time.

Prevention and Control of Air Pollution

Since the air pollutants could be gaseous or particulate, different techniques are used to control these pollutants.

A. Methods to Control Gaseous Pollutants

1. *Combustion*. This technique is useful when the pollutants are in the form of organic gases or vapours.
   - The organic pollutants are converted into water vapour and relatively less harmful gases like CO_2, by flame combustion or a catalytic process.
2. *Absorption*. It is useful in removing pollutants present in gaseous effluents.
   - Gaseous effluents are passed through absorbers or scrubbers.
   - Absorbers contain a suitable liquid absorber that absorbs or modifies one or more pollutants present in the gaseous effluent.
3. *Adsorption*. Adsorption means absorption only at the surface.
   - In this case gaseous effluent is passed through a solid adsorbent.
   - The organic and inorganic pollutants present in effluent gases get adsorbed at the interface or surface of the solid adsorbent.

B. Methods to Control Particulate Emissions

Device	*Methods*
1. *Mechanical devices*	Mechanical devices work on the basis of following principles: (a) *Gravity*. The separation is done by the particle size of the pollutant. The particles settle down by the gravitation force in the gravity settling tanks. (b) *Sudden change in the direction* of the gas flow. A sudden directional change causes the particles to separate out due to greater momentum. The small particles are separated by cyclone collector (Fig. 4.6)
2. *Fabric filters*	In this the gases containing particulate matter and dust are made to pass through a *porous medium*. • The porous medium is a woven or filled fabric that acts like a filter. • The particulate matter from the gas gets trapped in the fabric filter and the clean gas passes out (Fig. 4.7)
3 *Wet scrubbers*	Wet scrubbers are used in chemical, metallurgical and mining industries to trap SO_2, NH_3 and metal fumes.
4. *Electrostatic precipitators*	In these, the gas containing dust, fumes, or aerosols is passed between two electrodes. • As the gas passes through charged electrodes, aerosol particles get precipitated on the electrode and settle down while the clean gas passes out (Fig. 4.8)

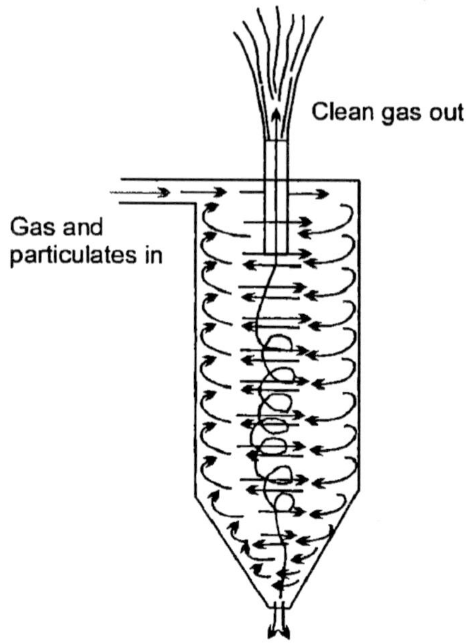

Fig. 4.6: Cyclone collector

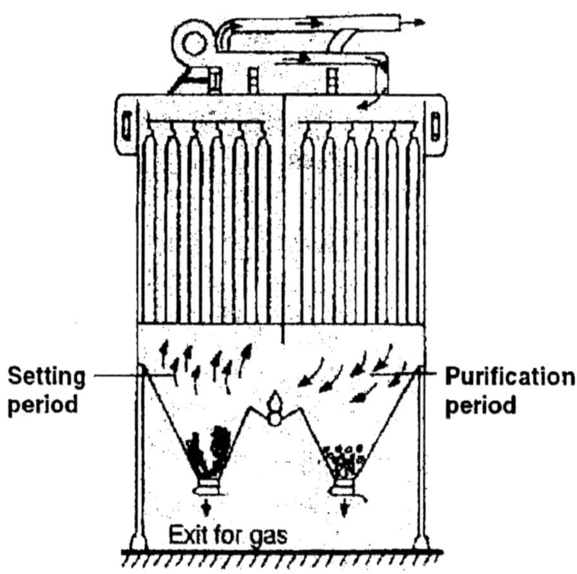

Fig. 4.7: A Typical Bag Filter

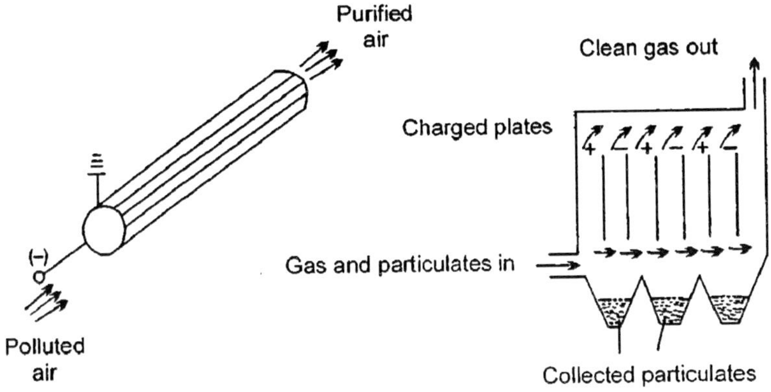

Fig. 4.8: A. Electrostatic Precipitator B. Plate Type Precipitator

Ways to Control Air Pollution

Air pollution can also be controlled by following ways.

1. By using better designed equipment and smokeless fuels like CNG (Compressed Natural Gas) or lead free petrol. Crude oil should be avoided to reduce SO_2, and hydrocarbons.
2. Automobiles should be properly maintained and fitted with exhaust emission controls like catalytic converters. They should follow emission control standards like Bharat II or Eruo II.
3. Increase in tree plantation can reduce CO_2 content of the environment.
4. Some renewable sources of energy like wind and solar energy and energy from ocean currents should be explored.
5. Tall chimneys should be installed for vertical dispersion of pollutants to avoid direct inhalation.
6. Enforcement of strict laws, monitoring pollution levels regularly and by imposing a check on pollutant causing materials. Industries should be located away from residential areas and should have filters to remove harmful pollutants from the gases.

WATER POLLUTION: SOURCES, CAUSES, EFFECTS AND CONTROLS

Water is the basic necessity of life. Recently water pollution has become a major concern all over the world.

Role of Water

(i) Water is a major component of the body cells and is essential for all life processes.
(ii) The energy of water falls, tides and oceans is used to *generate power* and move the machines.
(iii) It is essential for agriculture and industry.
(iv) Rivers and oceans provide a surface for navigation and shipping.

Freshwater is renewable but becoming scarce due to pollution. Freshwater is a renewable resource. The water evaporates from water bodies (oceans, rivers and lakes) and forms clouds. The water vapour in clouds subsequently cools and condenses to form rain or snow and fills up the water bodies again. Though water is a renewable source, it is unequally distributed on earth. The rain and snow vary with altitude and latitude causing floods in some and droughts in other areas.

Clean drinking freshwater is becoming more scarce than ever before. The freshwater that is available is also getting polluted by inorganic, organic and biological agents. The limited available water is becoming unfit for use.

Portable or drinking water is the one that is:

(i) Transparent, colourless and odourless.
(ii) Contains sufficient dissolved oxygen.
(iii) Free from harmful chemicals.
(iv) Free from any pathogens or coliform bacteria.

Polluted Water

Water is said to be polluted when there is physical, chemical or biological change.

- Physical change means change in its colour or turbidity.
- Chemical change means pollution by inorganic or organic substances, like fertilisers, excreta, cleaning agents, heavy metals etc.
- Biological change means addition of any harmful bacteria, viruses, animal or plants.

The polluted water is unfit for drinking and adversely affects living organisms.

Sources of Water Pollution

Water can get polluted from a number of sources which can be broadly classified as:

(i) Point sources
(ii) Non-point sources.

Sources and Causes Water Pollution

(1) Point sources	(2) Non-point sources
• Sources of pollution close to water source	• Sources of pollution are scattered and do not have any specific location.
• They discharge pollutants directly into water source	• No specific location to discharge the pollutants. Pollutants are discharged at various places.
• It is generally possible to treat the pollutants before they enter the water body	• Generally it is difficult to monitor, regulate and treat the pollutants before they enter the water body.
Examples: Factories; power plants; Underground coal mines, oil wells situated close to water source.	*Examples*: Lawns, gardens, construction sites; roads, streets, runoff from fields, water from water logging areas etc.

Major Water Pollutants

Given below in Table 4.3 are some of the major pollutants of water and their sources:

Table 4.3: Major Water Pollutants and Their Sources

Major water pollutants	*Their sources*
(i) Compounds of calcium and magnesium	They get dissolved from natural deposits in and around water sources.
Inorganic nitrates and phosphates	From fertilisers and pesticides
(ii) Micro-organisms like disease causing bacteria, viruses and protozoans,	From animal excreta, runoff water from pits, septic tanks, refuse dumps etc.
(iii) Oil, grease, petroleum products	From oil tankers while being loaded or unloaded.
(iv) Heavy metals	From industrial wastes and effluents.
(v) Detergents	From domestic cleaning agents, soap factories etc.
(vi) Domestic waste	From household wastes.
(vii) Hot water and radioactive waste	From electric, thermal and nuclear power plants.

Harmful Effects of Water Pollution

1. Polluted water causes a number of water-borne diseases like jaundice, cholera, typhoid, dysentery, hepatitis, diarrhoea etc., in man.
2. The acids or alkalis present in water destroy certain micro-organisms, thereby hindering the self-purification process in rivers.
3. Water polluted with fertilizers containing nitrates and phosphates causes eutrophication in water bodies.
   Eutrophication
   - It refers to a condition caused by a sudden increase in the amounts of nutrients in a lake or pond whereby there is a sudden algal growth (algal bloom)
   - *Sudden increase in the growth of green plants mainly algae* forms a dense cover on the surface of the lake.
   - This excessive growth *depletes the oxygen* dissolved in water. Also as algae begin to die after completion of their life cycle, they are decomposed by bacteria which also use up most of oxygen of water.
   - The reduction of dissolved oxygen leads to *death of most fish and other animals* for lack of O_2.
   - This destruction may take many years for a lake to recover.
4. Poisonous industrial wastes discharged in water lead to mass destruction of aquatic life including fishes. This directly affects the source of food for man.
5. A number of pesticides (like DDT) have residues like organochlorine compounds that persist for a long time and are very harmful. They make their way to man through food chain and accumulate in the fatty tissues. They affect nervous system severely.
6. Oil slick in sea water causes death of sea birds either by poisoning or by sticking together of feathers. It kills most of the plants and animals in oceans especially the coastal areas.

Table 4.4: Some Major Water Pollutants and Their Effects on Human Health

Water pollutants	*Effects on human health*
1. Domestic sewage contains pathogens like virus, bacteria parasitic protozoa and worms	Contaminated water carries germs of water-bone diseases like jaundice, cholera, typhoid, amoebiasis etc. (*This contaminated water is unfit for drinking, bathing and swimming*)
2. Heavy metal-mercury (Hg)	Mercury poisoning causes (*Minamata disease*) due to consumption of fish captured from mercury contaminated water. • It was first detected in the Minamata Bay in Japan in 1952, as people there suffered from this disease by consuming fish captured from mercury-contaminated Minamata Bay • Mercury compounds in waste waterget converted into extremely toxic methyl mercury by bacterial action. These compounds affect the nervous system and cause: — numbness of limbs, lips and tongue — deafness — blurring of vision — mental derangement
3. Cadmium	Causes *itai-itai* disease (ouch-ouch disease, a painful disease of bones and joints). — Also causes cancer of liver and lung.
4. Excess nitrate in drinking water	Extremely dangerous for human health. Can be fatal for infants. • Causes *Methaemoglobinemia* or *blue-baby syndrome*. — Nitrates react with haemoglobin and form non-functional *methaemoglobin*. — Methaemoglobin impairs oxygen transport in the body as it cannot carry oxygen. This leads to oxygen deprivation of the body and the body turns blue.
5. Excess floride in drinking water	— Leads to dental disorders and neuro-muscular disease. — Causes hardened bones and stiff and painful joints called *skeletal fluorosis*.
6. Arsenic in water	Chronic (long-term) exposure to arsenic causes *black-foot disease*. — Arsenic poisoning also causes diarrhoea, peripheral neurites and hyperkeratosis. Also causes skin and lung cancers

Prevention and Control of Water Pollution

A number of methods can be adopted to control water pollution.

1. *Sewage Disposal.* Sewage facilities to be made available in the houses. Sewage should be treated before it is discharged into the river or ocean. It can be done by making use of modern techniques.
2. *Recycling of Pollutants.* Various pollutant wastes can be recycled instead of dumping into water. For example, waste food material, paper, decaying vegetables and plastics etc., should be collected in separate bins for recycling and not thrown into open drains.
3. *Treatment of Industrial Effluents.* The effluents from distilleries, solid factory wastes containing organic matter should be sent to bio gas plants for generation of energy. The sewage and other factory waste should be treated before discharging into waterways.
4. *Oil Slicks in Oceans should be Skimmed Off* from the surface of water with suction devices. Saw dust may be spread over oil slick to absorb oil.

Treatment of Sewage

Sewage is treated in steps/stages as given below:

1. *First Step or Primary Treatment.* In this step, *large and suspended particles are removed*

(i) Sewage is passed through a grinding mechanism.

(ii) Next, it is passed through several settling chambers and neutralised with lime.

At this state sewage still contains a large number of pathogenic and non-pathogenic organism and also a large quantity of organic matter.

2. *Second Step or Secondary Treatment also called Biological Treatment.* In this step the bacterial activity decomposes the organic waste material present in the water.

(i) The neutralised effuents are now sent to a reactor called *upflow anaerobic sledge blanket (UASB).*

- In this treatment anaerobic bacteria decompose the

biodegradable material present in the waste. This process:

(a) removes the foul odour.

(b) releases methane gas that can be used elsewhere.

(c) reduces the pollution of water by 85 per cent.

(ii) Now the water is sent to *aeration tanks* where water is mixed with air and *bacteria.*

- Aerobic bacteria digest the organic waste material.

After this stage also water is not fit for drinking since a number of harmful micro-organisms still remain.

3. *Third Step or Tertiary Treatment.* It is disinfection process:

- to remove final traces of organic matter.
- to remove harmful bacteria and other micro-organisms.
- to remove dissolved inorganic solids etc.

In this step a number of methods are employed like chlorination, evaporation and exchange absorption.

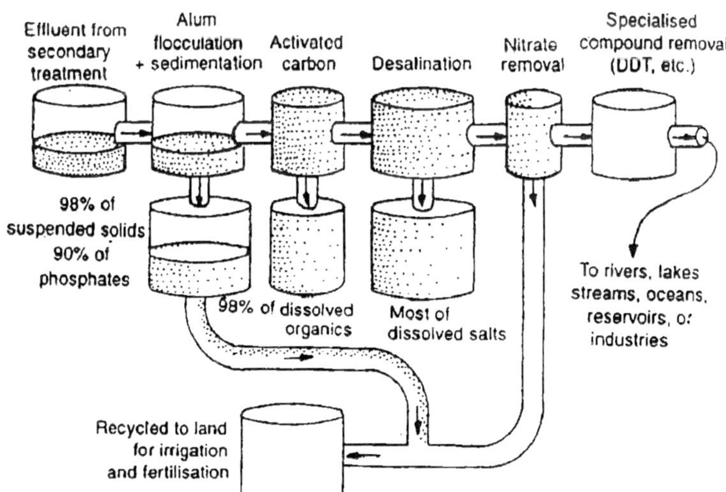

Fig. 4.9: Representation of Tertiary Treatment in an Effluent Treatment Plant

LAND POLLUTION: CAUSES, SOURCES, EFFECTS AND CONTROL

Land is the solid portion of the earth's surface. Soil forms the topmost layer of the land surface. About 4/5th of the land area is covered by soil.

Land pollution is mainly due to *solid waste*. Certain chemicals like *compounds of sulphur and lead* discharged into air, finally settle down and come to soil and pollute it.

1. Sources of Solid Waste

Solid waste that pollutes the land comes from various sources.

- A large part of solid waste comes from the houses, cattle sheds, industries, agricultural fields.
- Solid waste if not cleared, accumulates in the form of heaps on the land surface.
- It includes wastes like ash, glass, paper, clothes, plastic, rubber, leather, brick, sand, metal, peels of fruits and vegetables, cattle shed, night soil, cow dung and other discarded wastes.

2. Harmful Effects of Solid Waste

(i) The heaps of solid waste make the surroundings dirty.

(ii) They destroy the natural beauty and damage the landscape. Recent expeditions to the Himalayan range have found tons of garbage littered on their way, spoiling the beauty and the landscape. With time it would affect the flora and fauna (plants and animals) of these areas as well.

(iii) Invariably whenever there is a garbage heap, animals like pigs, dogs, rats and cows visit it and litter the garbage all around, making it an *unhealthy site*.

(iv) Garbage pollutes the surroundings by giving *foul smell*.

(v) Garbage dumps are breeding grounds of bacteria, flies and mosquitoes which are carriers of a number of diseases in man like cholera, diarrhoea etc.

(vi) Many a time wastes block the flow of water in the drain, and become an ideal breeding ground for mosquitoes, the carriers of malarial parasite that cause malaria.

3. Modes of Waste Disposal

To save land pollution, it is necessary to adopt techniques for safe disposal of wastes. The technique of disposal depends on the type of waste. Some of these are as given on next page:

Type of waste	*Technique of waste disposal*
1. Most solid wastes (domestic as well as industrial solid waste).	Used as landfills in urban area.
2. Some solid waste like plastics, metals and papers.	Can be sent for recycling.
• Plastic bags, buckets, bowls, mugs, dishes, plates, tables etc.	These materials can be taken up for recycling so that they can be reused.
• Scrap metal and industrial metallic waste.	Metal can also be melted and recycled into solid metal again.
3. Molten plastic waste from industries.	The molten plastic waste mixed with asphalt can be used for road construction.
4. Most domestic waste containing biodegradable organic waste.	Can be used to prepare manure for plants (manures are highly cost effective and cost much less than chemical fertilisers).
• Cow dung and other wastes	Can be used to prepare biogas also
5. Industrial toxic wastes.	These are treated in special waste disposal plants.

Volume of waste can be reduced by burning it at a very high temperature (incineration) in an incinerator (Fig. 4.10).

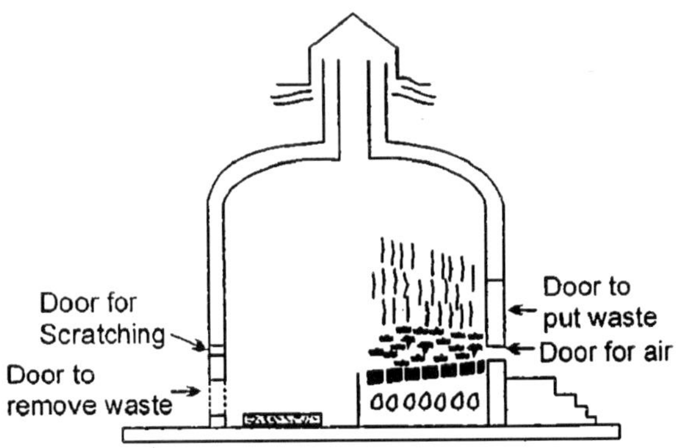

Fig. 4.10: Incinerator

4. Management of Solid Wastes

Management of solid wastes involves:

(i) Collection of biodegradable and non-biodegradable wastes in separate bags.

(ii) Disposable of these wastes separately.
(iii) Recovery of certain things like scrap metal, plastic etc., from the waste for recycling and reuse.
(iv) Safe disposal of toxic wastes with minimum environmental pollution.

SOIL EROSION

Soil. Soil forms the top-most layer of the land surface. About 4/5th of the land area is covered by soil. Soil takes thousands, sometimes millions of years to form. Human activities like removal of vegetations, ill planned urbanisation, felling of trees for human habitation and expansion of urban areas lead to exposure of top soil to wind and water.

Functions of Soil

(i) Soil provides anchorage to plants.
(ii) It is a source of water and mineral nutrition or terrestrial plants.
(iii) Dead animals and plants get decayed in soil. Number of decomposers like bacteria and fungi inhabit the soil that helps in recycling of nutrients.

Composition of Soil. Soil is a complex mixture of living and non-living materials. It is made up of mineral matter, decomposed remains of organic matter (human), living organisms like bacteria, fungi, algae etc., air and water.

1. Causes of Soil Erosion

1. *Natural agents* like water and wind constantly remove the top soil from land and cause soil erosion. Plant cover significantly reduces soil erosion. *Human activities* like cutting of trees, deforestation and over grazing remove the natural plant cover. Rain falling on unprotected topsoil erodes the soil as it cannot hold water and the eroded soil gets washed away into streams, rivers and lakes.
2. *Dust storm* also causes tremendous soil erosion. It picks up the top soil in such large quantities that it forms the clouds of dust and carries them away with force.
3. *Improper* tilling also causes soil erosion. Often farmers loosen

the top soil for various activities like removing of weeds and preparation of seed beds etc. Then they leave their fields for a long time till the onset of right season for the crop. During this time soil is prone to soil erosion by strong winds or rains.

Direct and Indirect Sources of Soil Pollution

Soil pollution can occur due to various direct and indirect reasons:

(i) *Direct*

(a) *Waste Dump.* Dumping of industrial, and medical wastes etc.

(b) *Municipal Waste.* Dumping of discarded wastes like paper, food, plastics, polyethylene bags etc.

(c) *Use of Agrochemicals.* Excess of agrochemicals in the form of pesticides, fertilisers etc.

(d) *Mining Operations.* Damage of soil by open mining activities.

(ii) *Indirect*

(a) By air pollution like acid rain.

(b) By water pollution like pollutants finding their way to soil.

2. Effects of Soil Pollutants

Soil pollution is mainly by human activities like waste dumping, use of agrochemicals, mining operations and urbanisation. Effects of the pollutants released by these activities are given in Table 4.5.

3. Prevention of Soil Erosion

Soil erosion can be checked by a number of means as given below:

1. *Restoring Forests and Grass Covers.* It needs planting of trees and sowing drought resistant grasses so that the soil is not left bare. A grass cover or vegetation cover is an excellent binding material that stops soil erosion.
2. *Contour Farming and Terracing* on the sloping fields reduces the speed of water flow. Hence, it checks the soil erosion.
3. *Intensive Cropping, Crop Rotation* (planting legumes in between cereal crops) and several other crop management practices can minimise soil erosion and save the soil from being depleted of nutrients.

Table 4.5: Effects of the Pollutants

Type of wastes	*Pollutants*	*Effects*
1. Waste Dumps		
(i) Industrial solid waste and sludge	Toxic organic and inorganic chemical compounds and heavy metals like salts of iron, lead, copper, mercury and arsenic.	Toxic to both plants and animals.
(ii) Industrial emissions	Fly ash from thermal power plants. Particulars matter emitted from tall chimney.	Pollute the surrounding land. Come back to earth sooner or later and pollute the soil.
(iii) Nuclear plants and nuclear testing laboratories	Radioactive wastes Radioactive fall out from nuclear explosions.	Contaminate soil with radioactive materials that remain in the soil for very long periods as they have long half-life. For example Strontium-90 has a half-life of 28 years and Caesium-137 has of 30 years. These substances make their way to plants and animals and cause serious damage. Refer radioactive pollution in section 21.9 of this chapter.
2. Municipal Wastes Municipal wastes, include domestic and kitchen wastes, market wastes, livestock and poultry wastes, waste metals etc.	Non-biodegradable wastes polythene carry bags, plastic sheets, pet bottles, metal needles, plastic and glass bottles, vials etc.	(i) Damage the landscape, create foul smell and destroy natural beauty. (ii) Present in the soil for very long periods. With time, affect flora and fauna.

(Contd.)

(*Contd.*)

Type of wastes	*Pollutants*	*Effects*
	Biodegradable wastes Discarded food, paper, excretory products of animals etc.	Number of pathogens present in the wastes contaminate the soil. Cause health hazards for men and domestic animals.
3. Agrochemicals Pet and weed control agricultural systems.	Pesticides, weedicides —Fertilisers and biocide residues (contain phosphates and nitrates)	(i) Contaminate the soil and cause death of micro-organisms; animals and certain plants. (ii) Contaminate the surface and ground water resources. (iii) Change chemical properties of soil and have damaging effects of soil organisms.
4. Mining Operation Opencast mining (a process where the surface of the earth is dug open to extract, out the underground mineral deposits)	Toxic metals and chemicals	Completely damage the land and pollute the top soil and contaminate the area with toxic metals and chemicals.

4. Instead of conventional tillage, the *residues from the previous crops should be left* in the soil. It not only checks soil erosion but also increases the organic matter of soil and improves the soil moisture capacity.
5. Flood prone and irrigated lands should have *adequate drainage* for easy flow of water.

NOISE POLLUTION—MEANING, CAUSES, SOURCES, EFFECTS AND CONTROL

Noise pollution is defined as *unwanted high pitched sound*. The concept of unwanted sound may differ with the people since sound or noise is an inseparable part of everyday life.

It has been proved that high intensity sound from various sources has damaging *physiological* and *psychological* effects.

Unit of Sound Intensity. Noise can be measured by the sound meter and is expressed in a unit called *decibel* (dB). This word was chosen to recognise the work of Alexander Grahm Bell.

- The quietest sound that the human ear can detect is called the *threshold of hearing*.
- Fig 4.11 gives the loudness of sounds as measured in decibels to a series of everyday situations.
- Note that a sound of 120 dB is on the *threshold of pain* (Fig. 4.11), i.e., sounds louder than this actually hurt your ears and can give a physical discomfort and headache.

If such a sound goes on continuously it can damage the sensory cells in the inner ear, causing permanent deafness. People who work close to machines in foundries or mills should wear ear-plugs as protection from high sound.

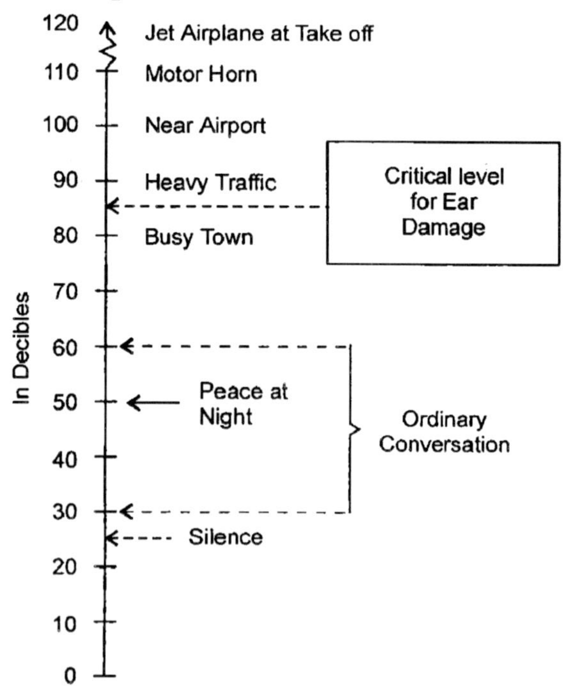

Fig. 4.11: Level of Sound Intensity

- In the scale of intensity, sound of 10, 20 and 100 decibels represents 10 times, 100 times and 10^{10} times the threshold of hearing intensity. The difference in the intensity by 10 dB means 10 times more the intensity.

  (10 db = 10 times; (10^1) 20 dB = 10 × 10 = 100 times; (10^2)
  30 d B = 10 × 10 × 10 times and so on). (10^3)

1. Sources of Noise Pollution

(i) Industrial machines like the ones used in textile mills, printing press, engineering establishments and defence equipment.
(ii) Transport vehicles like trains, buses, scooters with blaring horns.
(iii) Dynamite blastings, bull dozers, excavators, lawnmowers give loud shrilling sounds.
(iv) Modern domestic gadgets like food blenders, coolers, exhaust fans, blaring radios, public address systems.
(v) Super sonic aeroplanes.
(vi) Experiments like rocket launching, explosions and firing produce deafening sound.

2. Effects of Noise Pollution

(i) Impairment of hearing-Lung exposure to loud noises (may be music) results in some hearing loss.
(ii) A noise level of 95 decibels may lead to stress, anxiety and nervous tension.
(iii) Unwanted sound may lead to increase in heart beat, constriction of blood vessels, dilation of the pupil of eye, nausea and fluctuations in blood pressure.
(iv) Sudden high intensity of sound may affect nervous system.
(v) Noise can influence unborn babies producing malformation of the foetal nervous system that may affect the behaviour later.
(vi) Along with physiological disorders, noise also causes serious psychological disorders.

3. Control of Noise Pollution

(i) Use of the better designed, quieter machines in industries.
(ii) Noise can be minimised by proper lubrication and better

maintenance. Sound proof jackets or filters can reduce noise from machines.

(iii) The workers should be made to wear protective devices like ear muffs or cotton plugs to reduce occupational exposure.

(iv) Noisy industries should be away from the residential areas.

(v) Big cities should enforce restriction on the use of loud speakers and amplifiers.

(vi) Plantation of coniferous trees on highways reduces the noise.

(vii) Strict enforcement of international regulations to use better designed engines for aeroplanes.

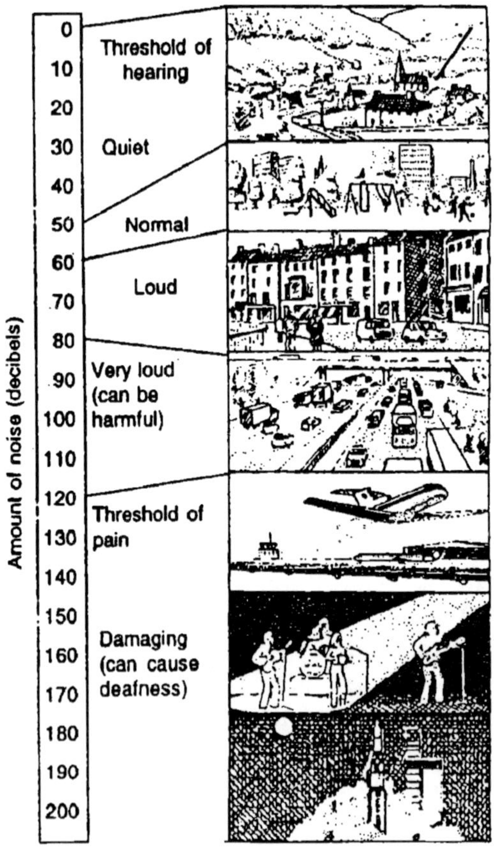

Fig. 4.12: A Schematic Representation Showing Noise Scale in Decibles (as measured with sound meter)

'Silent Zone' around 100 metres of hospitals or schools can give comfort to ailing patients or help students to concentrate in studies. Table 4.6 for the permissible noise levels in various zones

Table 4.6: Zonewise Permissible Ambient Noise Levels

Zones	*Day*	*Night*
	(0600-2100hrs 6 a.m. – 9 p.m.	(2100-0600 hrs 9 p.m. – 6 a.m.
1. Industry	75dB	70dB
2. Commercial	65dB	55dB
3. Residential	55dB	45dB
4. Silent Zone (like hospitals and schools)	50dB	40dB

4. Environmental Laws for Controlling Pollution

Given below are some of the important Acts that deal with the protection of environment in India.

(i) *The Insecticide Act, 1968.* This Act deals with the regulation of import, manufacture, sale, transport, distribution and use of insecticides with a view to prevent risk to human health and other organisms.

(ii) *The Waste (Prevention and Control of Pollution) Act, 1974.* This Act deals with the preservation of water quality and the control of water pollution with a concern for the detrimental effects of water pollutants on human health and also on the biological world.

(iii) *The Air (Prevention and Control of Pollution) Act, 1981.* This Act deals with the prevention of air quality and the control of air pollution with a concern for the detrimental effects of air pollution on human health and on the biological world.

(iv) *The Environment (Protection) Act, 1986.* This Act deals with the *protection of air, water* and *soil* quality, and the control of environmental pollutants including noise pollution.

Amendment in 1987 to the Air Act 1981 – In 1987, in the Air Act 1981, noise as an air pollutant was also added.

RADIOACTIVE POLLUTION: MEANING, CAUSES, SOURCES, EFFECTS AND CONTROL

Radioactive pollution is a kind of physical pollution that affects all life supporting systems like water, land and air.

Definition. Radioactivity is a phenomenon of spontaneous emission of protons (a particles), electron (b particles) and short wave electromagnetic waves (g particles) as a result of disintegration of atomic nuclei of some elements.

1. Kinds of Radioactive Pollution

(i) *Natural Source.* It comprises of *cosmic rays* coming from space and terrestrial radiations from *radio nuclides* present in the earth's crust occurring naturally in rocks, soil an water. Examples of radio nuclides are Radium 224, Uranium 235, Uranium 238, Thorium 232, Radon 222, Potassium 40 and Carbon 14.

(ii) *Man-made Sources.* These are a result of many man-made activities like:

(a) Mining and refining of plutonium and thorium.

(b) Production and explosion of nuclear weapons.

(c) Nuclear power plants producing nuclear energy.

(d) Preparation of radioactive isotopes like C^{14}, P^{32}, S^{35}.

Though man has always been exposed to low levels of radiation from natural sources for several million years, now the danger has increased due to man-made sources.

2. Nuclear Weapons

The nuclear weapons were used in the form of *atomic bombs* during Second World War. The first bomb was exploded in Nagasaki and the second in Hiroshima (Japan, 1945). They caused huge devastation of innocent people, animals and plants.

Even today the craze for acquiring more and more of nuclear weapons by big powers is continuing unabated. At present there is enough stock-pile to destroy the complete earth.

How is Nuclear Energy Produced?

Large unstable nuclei of some atoms like Uranium 238 have a tendency to break up on their own (though found rarely in natural conditions). If Uranium 238 is *bombarded* with a slow moving neutron, splitting of uranium occurs which is known as *fission*. It is in the form of a chain reaction. During the fission, a large amount of *nuclear energy* is released in the form of *heat* along with α, β and γ rays.

Energy by fission of 1 kg of uranium = Energy obtain by 900,000 kg of coal.

Nuclear Reaction

The chain reaction gives rise to large number of neutrons which make other materials like Strontium 90, Iodine 131 also radioactive. The radioactive materials transformed into gases with immense heat, rise in the sky like a mushroom cloud.

3. Spread of Radioactivity

(i) The radioactive particles are carried away by wind to very far off areas that are miles apart.
(ii) The particles settle down and cause water and soil pollutions that are thousands of miles away from the site of explosion.
(iii) The rain drops may contain radioactive particles and transfer them to soil particles.
(iv) From the soil, radioactive elements reach various animals through the food chain.
(v) Aquatic animals may absorb it directly or through food chain which also may ultimately include man.

4. Sources of the Radioactive Pollution

(i) *Nuclear Reactors and Nuclear Fuel*
  (a) The nuclear fuel as well as the coolants have radioactive substances.
  (b) The radioactive wastes contain activation products.
  (c) Inert gases and halogens that may escape from nuclear reactors contain radioactive particles.
  (d) People working in nuclear reactors may get it accidently.

(ii) *Research Labs*
Radio isotopes like C^{14}, I^{125}, P^{32} are widely used as tracer molecules in biochemistry labs. The waste waters may reach the river and lakes through sewers.

(iii) *Food Chain*
Aquatic animals, slimes, sludges, microorganisms, herbivores like cattle grazing on polluted fields ultimately

pass them to other organisms of food chain.

(iv) *Radiation Therapy*
Human beings voluntarily receive them in limited controlled doses as a cure or for diagnostic purpose.
- X-rays are used for understanding various human ailments.
- Radioactive iodine is used for curing goitre.
- Radiation therapy is used for cancer.

Effects of Radioactive Pollution

Radioactive pollution affects both plants and animals.

(i) In higher doses it causes instant deaths.
(ii) In lower doses it can affect all organs seriously and impair their functions.
(iii) Long or repeated exposure can cause cancer and leukaemia and may induce mutations.
(iv) The mutated genes can persist in the organism and the effects are passed on to the offspring.
In Japan, handicapped children were born to mothers exposed to radiations even after many years.

The Effect of a Radioactive Pollutant Depends Upon the Following Aspects

(i) *Half Life*. Time needed for half of its atoms to decay. This can vary from a fraction of a second to thousands of years.
(ii) Energy releasing capacity.
(iii) Rate of diffusion.
(iv) Rate of deposition of the contaminant.
(v) Climatic conditions like wind, temperature, rainfall etc.

Control of Radioactive Pollution

Since the radioactive materials are used in many effective ways like propulsion of big ships, for biological and medicinal studies, curing of cancer and tumours, in agriculture, biochemistry, for preservation of food and dating of archaeological remains, we cannot do away with them. As there is no cure for radiation damage, prevention is the only safest way.

Management of Toxic Chemicals and Hazardous Wastes

Every year, between 1000 and 2000 new organic and inorganic

chemicals are produced. This brings the total of commercially-produced chemicals to substantially more than 1000,000, many of which are toxic.

Toxic chemicals are released directly into the environment, for example, as pesticides or fertilisers, and indirectly as wastes from other activities such as mining, industrial processes incineration and fuel combustion.

Worldwide, some 338 million tones of hazardous wastes are produced every year, mostly in the industrialised countries—275 millions in the North America and 25 Millions in Western Europe. Much of this hazardous waste has been deposited in landfills or stored in surface impoundments where leaks have contaminated groundwater and soil. As industrialised countries have tightened their controls over the movement and disposal of hazardous wastes, illegal dumping and traffic has increased. In the last 1980s, a series of scandals came to light, involving hazardous waste dumping in developing countries (Source: UNEP).

SUMMARY: IMPORTANT POINTS

1. *Pollution is an undesirable change* in our soundings. It is a result of human activity and affects air, land and water. With the Industrial Revolution, it has become a major threat to mankind.
2. *Pollutants* that can be broken down by micro-organisms are called *biodegradable* while the ones that cannot be broken down an *non-biodegradable.*
3. *Air pollution* could be due to gaseous or particulate pollutants which could be emitted due to natural activities like volcanic eruption, forest fires or dust storms or due to the activities of man like automobiles, pesticides, deforestation and use of CFCs etc.
4. *Air pollution* can be due to primary pollutants like SO_2, SO_3, NO_2 CFCs pollen grains, dust or due to secondary pollutants like nitrous compounds and *PAN*.
5. Many products of incomplete combustion undergo photochemical reactions with oxides of nitrogen to generate smog which is found hanging over many industrialised nations.
6. Various industries, mining activities, automobiles and

agricultural industries release *harmful gases* and huge quantities of *particulate pollutants*.

7. Increased CO_2 is causing a green house effect. It is responsible for the rise in temperature on the Earth.
8. Pollutants like CFCs are the causes of depletion of ozone layer that protects earth from intense UV rays of Sun.
9. Many other pollutants especially in industrialised areas are causing respiratory and vascular disorders. Some like hydrocarbons are carcinogenic. They affect the vegetation and other animals as well.
10. Atmospheric pollution which is posing a threat to the climatic and atmospheric stability needs to be controlled.
11. Different techniques can be adopted to control different pollutants.
12. *Gaseous pollutants* can be controlled by combustion, absorption or adsorption techniques.
13. *Particulate pollutants* can be controlled by mechanical devices like gravity or sudden change in the direction of flow, by fabric filters, wet scrubbers or by electrostatic precipitators.
14. *Freshwater* gets polluted by domestic sewage, pesticides, fertilisers, and industrial wastes.
15. The *underground water* is getting polluted by seepage of sewage or industrial/waste.

5

Environmental Hazards

Global and Local Causes and Effects

MEANING OF GLOBAL ENVIRONMENTAL HAZARDS

In simple words global environment hazards mean imbalances in the environment of the world.

To cater to the needs of huge population and due to the advancement in science and technology, human beings are trying to manipulate the environment. In doing so, they have caused environmental imbalance and a number of environmental problems like:

- — Conversion of forests to grazing lands or croplands by deforestation has caused loss of carbon stored in soil and vegetation to the atmosphere, ultimately affecting the global carbon cycle.
- — Biomass burning associated with agricultural practices releases large amount of CO_2 in the atmosphere.
- — Increased number of automobiles on roads and use of aerosols and other substances releasing CFCs add methane (CH_4), Nitrous oxide (N_2O) and CFCs to the lower atmosphere.

The above mentioned gases CO_2, CH_4, N_2O and CFCs called *radiatively active gases*, also called *green house gases* can absorb long wave infra-red radiations. The presence of increased amount of these gases are causing the changes in the *global climate* or environmental changes at the global scale.

THE GREENHOUSE EFFECT AND GLOBAL WARMING

1. The Greenhouse Effect

The earth's temperature is maintained by the balance of incoming

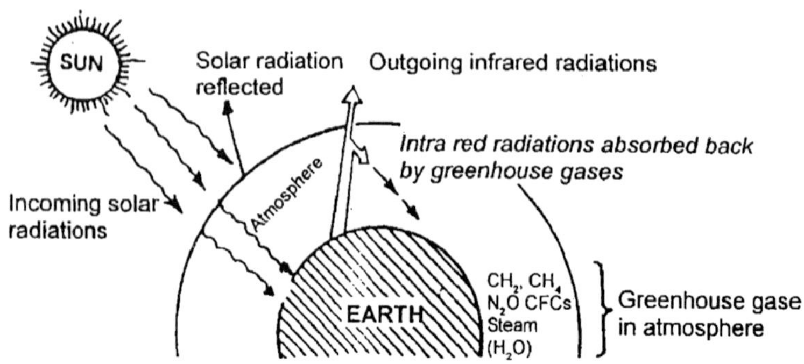

Fig. 5.1: Greenhouse effect; CO_2 and other atmospheric gases absorb the radiations and hence inhibit the escape of total radiation

and outgoing solar radiations. Radiations from sun pass through the atmosphere and are reflected back into space.

The atmosphere acts like the window glasspane of a gigantic greenhouse surrounding the earth.

Carbon dioxide (CO_2) and other atmospheric gases like methane (CH_4), nitrous oxide (N_2O), CFC, and water vapour (H_2O) inhibit the escape of total radiation. They absorb long wave or infrared radiations and so all the solar radiations reaching the planet are not returned to outer space but a part of them are held back. *This blocking of part of the radiation (infra-red) and its reflection back towards the surface of the earth is known as the Greenhouse effect.* The atmospheric greenhouses form a blanket over the earth, control the escape of heat from the earth's surface to outer space and keep the earth warm.

Greenhouse Flux. This downward flux of infra-red radiations towards earth is called greenhouse flux. It keeps the earth warm.

Greenhouse Gases. Carbondioxide (CO_2); Methane (CH_4); Nitrous oxide (N_2O); Chloro fluoro carbon (CFCs) and water vapour (H_2O):

Greenhouse gases are also called *radioactively active gases* because they can absorb long wave infra-red radiation.

Effect of Greenhouse Gases on Earth's Temperature

— The mean annual temperature of earth is about 15°C.

— In the-absence of greenhouse gases in the atmosphere, the earth's means temperature would be around –20°C.

— More concentration of greenhouse gases means more temperature of earth.

What is a Greenhouse?

A greenhouse is an enclosed glass chamber in which temperature is kept higher than outside.

The greenhouses are used for growing plants that need higher temperatures for growth.

Enhanced Greenhouse Effect

Human activities have always had an effect on the climate. But with the industrialisation of many parts of the planet, the effects have multiplied. The industrial activities release tons of CO_2 into the atmosphere, along with hundreds of millions of tons of other "greenhouse gases" such as methane and the chloro-fluoro-carbon,

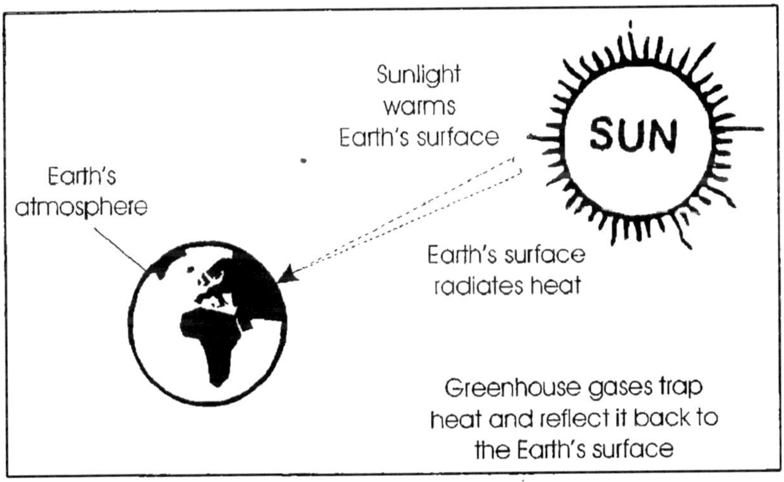

Fig. 5.2: The Greenhouse Effect

Energy from the Sun is either transmitted, reflected or trapped by the atmosphere. Energy radiated back into space is of longer wavelengths (in the infra-red region) than the energy arriving from the Sun, and the consequence is that more heat enters than can escape. Greenhouse gases (CO_2, CH_4, nitrous oxides, CFCs), together with water vapour in clouds, contribute to the 'blanketing' effect of the atmosphere.

as a result their presence in the atmosphere has increased tremendously. Forest fires also contribute considerably to the emission of "greenhouse gases."

Once released into the atmosphere, CO_2 remains there for a period of between 50 and 200 years. CH_4 on the other hand, remains for only 10 years, but can absorb between 20 and 30 times as much heat as CO_2.

The excessive increase in the concentration of greenhouses in the atmosphere would retain more and more of the infra-red radiations, resulting in the *enhanced greenhouse effect.*

This makes the temperature of the Earth's crust increase above the limits of the natural variations. Detailed scientific analysis have shown that the average global temperature of the Earth's surface has increased by 0.5 degrees in the last 100 years.

If emissions of "greenhouse gases" continue increasing at their current rate, then by the middle of the next century the temperature could reach the highest level in the last 20,000 years affecting the weather and climate of the world.

Fig. 5.3: Industrial Emission

GLOBAL WARMING

As a result of enhanced greenhouse effect, the consequent increase in the global mean temperature is called global warming. The Intergovernmental Panel on Climate Change IPCC periodically makes an assessment of the abundance of greenhouse gases in the atmosphere and their possible impact on climate and related issues.

Increased Concentration of Greenhouse Gases, Especially CO_2 and Global Warming

The natural greenhouse warming, caused mainly by carbon dioxide (CO_2) and water vapour is spiralling out of control as a result of human activities. With the industrialisation, every year industrial activities release almost 6,000 million tones of CO_2 into the atmosphere, along with other "greenhouse gases" such as methane, so that their presence in the atmosphere is increased massively. Their concentration are now 25 per cent higher than in pre-industrial times and are rising by 0.5 per cent every year.

Detailed scientific studies have shown that the average global temperature of the earth's surface has increased by 0.5°C in the last 100 years. If emission of "greenhouse gases" continue increasing at this current rate, the earth could heat up to 0.3°C each decade (10 years). Over the next century this would mean a warming of between 2°–5°C, a change that has not taken place in past 10,000 years. This can have unsettling effect on the climate of the earth. Global warming will have considerable effect on the earth's climate.

CO_2 is the Main Factor

It is estimated that CO_2 is responsible for 50 per cent of the increase in the greenhouse effect. Most of the CO_2 released into the atmosphere is a result of burning fossil fuels, so that if we want to reduce emissions of this gas we must first reduce the amount of coal, oil and natural gas we burn. It is also very important to burn these substances as efficiently as possible.

A large part of the energy consumed in the world today is not used to provide services from energy (heat, light, comfort, etc.), but is simply degraded in the form of non-usable heat.

Source: UNESCO

3. Relative Abundance of Greenhouse Gases

The trends in the increase in concentration of greenhouse gases since pre-industrial times are briefly described below:

1. *Carbon dioxide (CO_2)*
   - The *most abundant* greenhouse gas in the atmosphere.
   - Its level has increased by 31 per cent due to industrialisation since 1750.

- The increase is largely due to fossil fuel burning, deforestation and change in land use.

2. *Methane (CH_4)*

- Methane concentration has more than *doubled* since 1750 as a result of industrialisation.
- Methane is basically a product of *incomplete decomposition*. It is produced by a group of bacteria called *methanogens* under anaerobic conditions.
- Major sources of methane include:
  (i) fresh water wet lands,
  (ii) enteric fermentation in cattle,
  (iii) flood rice fields, and
  (iv) bio-mass burning.

3. *Nitrous Oxide(N_2O)*

- Concentration of N_2O in atmosphere has increased by 17 per cent due to industrialisation.
- Main sources of N_2O are (i) agriculture, (ii) bio-mass burning, (iii) industrial processes, N_2O is also produced during, (iv) burning of nitrogen-rich fuel, (v) livestock waste, (vi) breakdown of nitrogen rich fertilisers in soil and (vii) nitrate contaminated ground water.

4. *Chloroflurocarbons (CFCs)*

- CFCs are non-toxic, non-inflammable, highly stable and synthetic gaseous compounds of carbon and halogens (chlorine and fluorine)
- Use of CFCs and hydroflourocarbons (HFCs) began in 20th century only, and in a short span of time they have made a significant impact in global warming.

Main source of CFCs and HCFs →
- Propellents in aerosol sprays
- Air conditioners and refrigerating units
- solvents in industrial units (like cleaning agents)
- Production of plastic foam (stryo foam) for packing of food etc.

Table 5.1: The Increase in the Concentrations of Greenhouse Gases in the Atmosphere as Affected by Human Activities

Greenhouse gases	*Pre-industrial Concentration ~ 1750 AD*	*Concentration in 2000 AD*	*Increase since~1750 AD %*	*Atmospheric life-time (years)*
Carbon dioxide (CO_2)	280 ppm	368 ppm	31	5–200
Methane (CH_4^+)	700 ppb	1750 ppb	151	12
Nitrous oxide (N_2O)	270 ppb	316 ppb	17	114
Chlorofluorocarbons (CFC-11)	0	282 ppt		45–260
Hydroflurocarbons (HFC-23)				

ppm—parts per million: ppb—parts per billion, ppt—parts per trillion.

CFCs are unreactive at the Earth's surface but break down altitudes of between 15 to 50 kms. The CFCs persist for 45 to 260 years or more in the atmosphere.

A number of industries produce chlorine and fluorine compounds especially the chlorofluorocarbons (CFCs)

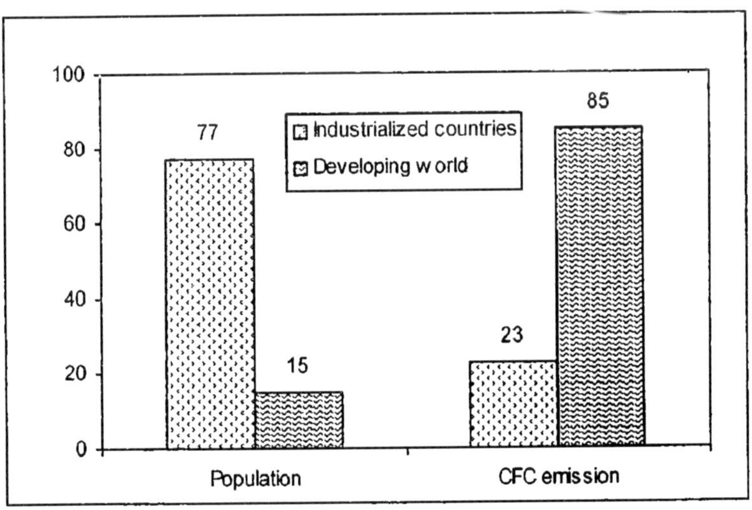

Fig. 5.4: Population and Pollution

CFCs damage the earth's ozone layer and contribute to global warming.

Clorofiuorocarbons (CFCs)

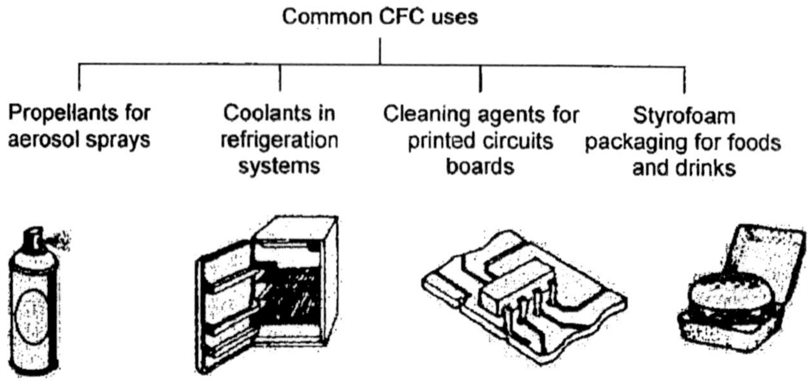

Fig. 5.5: Common CFC Uses

In the early 1930s, when they were first commercialised, CFCs (chlorofluorocarbons) seemed almost too good to be true. The most common CFCs are simple chemical structures and cheap to manufacture. They are made up of chlorine, fluorine and carbon atoms. Furthermore, they are non-toxic and inert, which means they do not combine easily with other substances.

Because they vaporise at low temperature CFCs act as ideal coolants in refrigerators and as propellant gases for spray cans containing anything from deodorants to insecticides. CFCs are also excellent for cleaning electrical circuit boards and are used to put the little bubbles in plastic-foam materials such as styrofoam. Today the annual market for CFCs is around US$ 2.2 billion.

However, by the end of the 1970s the world had become aware that the protective ozone shield in the atmosphere was endangered by CFCs and halons, gases used in fire extinguishers. In fact, the ozone layer was already greatly depleted in a huge 'hole' over the frozen part of Antarctica.

Until then the general public was largely unaware of an ozone shield, let alone the threat that CFCs represented to it. Human experience of ozone was as a toxic component of smog hanging over crowded cities. But in the upper atmosphere ozone takes on a life-sustaining role, protecting plant and animal life from excessive exposure to highly dangerous ultraviolet light (UV). At the upper reaches of the Earth's atmosphere, under intense ultraviolet bombardment from the sun, molecules of oxygen (O_2) are split into single atoms. Some of these single oxygen atoms rejoin existing molecules to form ozone (O_3). Ozone is dispersed throughout the stratosphere (15–50 km above the Earth's surface), stopping most of the sun's UV rays. Ozone exists in minute quantities especially over oceans. If it is compressed it would be thin as a window glass pane.

RELATIVE CONTRIBUTION OF DIFFERENT GREENHOUSE GASES TO GLOBAL WARMING

Contribution of various greenhouses on the total global warming are as given below and in Fig. 5.6.

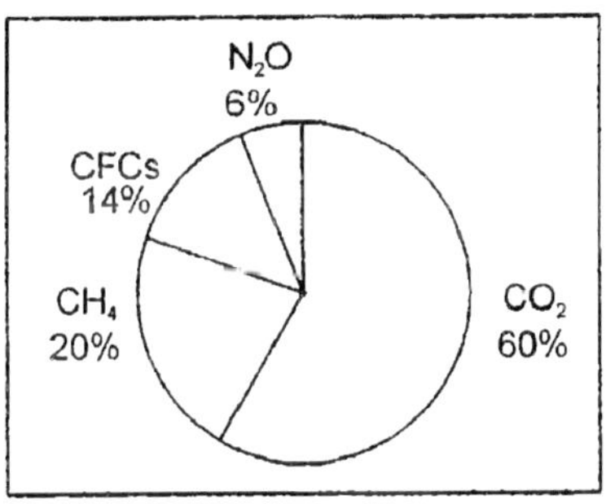

Fig. 5.6: The Relative Contribution of Different Greenhouse Gases due to Global Warming

EFFECTS OF ABUNDANCE OF GREENHOUSE GASES

The increase in the concentration of greenhouse gases have the following possible effects:

1. CO_2 'fertilisation effect' on plants
2. Global warming
3. Depleting of ozone layer in stratosphere.

1. CO_2 fertilisation Effect on Plants

Based on the data from Mauna Loa Observatory, USA, the level of CO_2 is rising tremendously.

In 1750, the atmospheric CO_2 concentration was 280 ppm.

In 2000, the atmospheric CO_2 concentration increased to about

368 ppm.

By the end of 21st century it is expected that the atmospheric CO_2 concentration shall increase to a level between 540 and 970 ppm i.e., double or triple or four times increase from pre-industrial time.

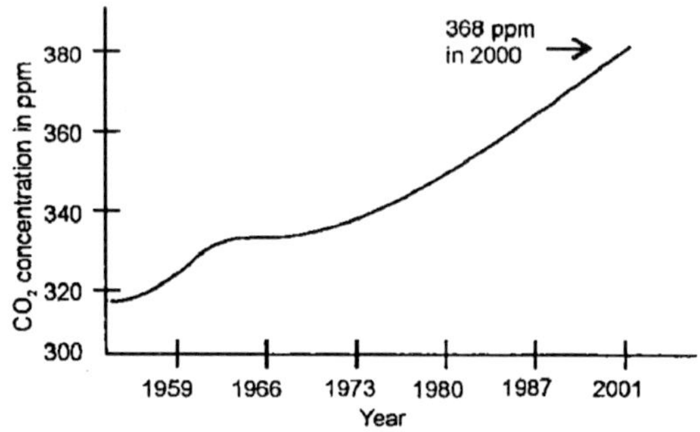

Fig. 5.7: The Increase in Mean carbon Dioxide Concentration in the Atmosphere from 1959 to 2001
(based on a data from Mauna Loa Observatory in Hawaii, USA).

Increase in CO_2 concentration has direct effect on the growth of C_3 plants.

In increased CO_2 concentration, under favourable conditions of water, temperature, light and nutrients, the growth in plants could increase by 30 per cent. This response of plants to higher CO_2 concentration is called *CO_2 fertilisation effect.* Due to increased CO_2 concentration, (i) the rate of photosynthesis will increase, (ii) the stomatal conductance will decrease. Thus the transpiration rate may be reduced and consequently water use efficiency will increase (iii) In higher CO_2 conditions plants may allocated greater proportion of photosynthates to roots, enhancing mycorrhizal development and more nitrogen fixation.

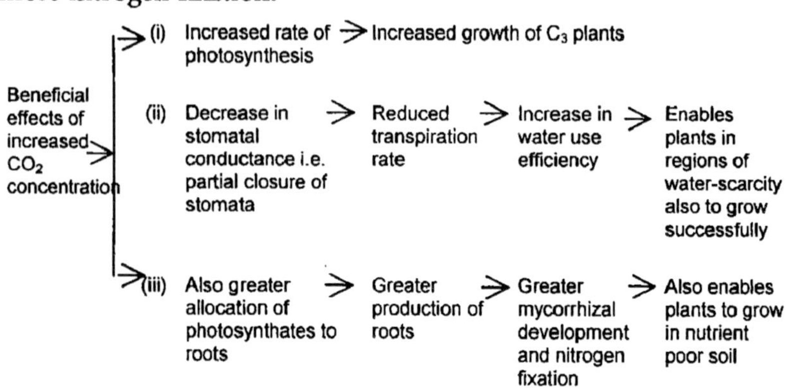

The above said beneficial effects of increased CO_2 concentration may not be actually realised due to negative effects of global warming.

- Beneficial effects of increased CO_2 concentration
  - (i) Increased growth of C_3 plants.
  - (ii) Plant species may grow successfully in regions of water scarcity.
  - (iii) Plants may grow in nutrient poor soil also.
- Negative effect of increased CO_2 concentration......Global warming.

POSSIBLE EFFECTS OF GLOBAL WARMING

Global warming refers to the increase in the global mean temperature which is due to the increase in concentration of 'greenhouse gases' (CO_2, CH_4, N_2O, CFCs) in the atmosphere.

The predicted global warming in near future will have a number of effects on earth. Some of these are:

1. Effects on weather and climate.
2. Rise in sea-level
3. Effect on species distribution
4. Effect on food production.

1. Effects on Weather and Climate

(i) The global mean temperature of earth has increased by app. 0.6°C in the 20th century.

- — Temperature of earth may increase by 1.4°C–5.8°C by the year 2100 from what it was in 1990.
- — The temperature changes will be most marked at the middle and high latitudes (at poles) than at the equator.
- — The Northern Hemisphere will warm more than the Southern Hemisphere because Northern Hemisphere has more land and land heats more quickly than water.

(ii) Warming of atmosphere will increase the moisture carrying capacity of air.

While the troposphere warms up, the stratosphere will cool down. This would cause changes in the precipitation patterns, due to changes in air mass movements.

- — It will lead to increased precipitation at higher altitude and lower precipitation at lower altitudes in winter.

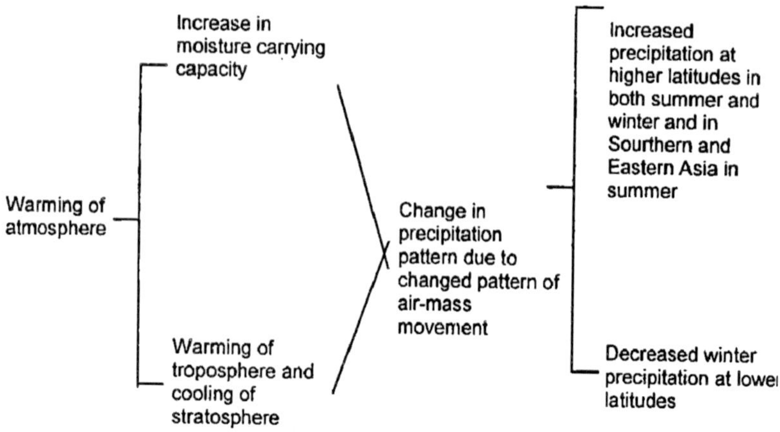

(iii) The frequency of extreme events like droughts and floods are expected to increase substantially.
  — More areas of the world would have extreme heat waves and more forest fires.

(iv) The climate change will increase the threat to human health due to changes in the vectors of diseases and water-borne pathogens, especially in the tropical and subtropical.

2. Effects on Sea Sevel/Discussed Separately

3. Effect on Species Distribution

The global warming is likely to change and shift the range of temperature over the globe.

(i) As both plant and animal species occur within a range of temperature, any temperature change would affect their distribution pattern attitudinally as well as latitudinally.

(ii) With global warming, many species are likely to shift slowly towards the pole (poleword) i.e. towards the high elevations of mountains.

For example. With a global rise in temperature of 2°–5°C during 21st century, the temperate region vegetation may extend 250–600 km poleward.

(iii) As trees are sensitive to temperature differences, rise in global temperature may lead to death of a large number of trees and their replacement by shrub vegetation.

(iv) Global warming may lead to extinction of a large number of plant and animal species.

4. Effects on Food Production

The increase in global temperature would bring about a number of changes in plants affecting food production like:

— Explosive growth of weeds.
— Eruption of a number of plant diseases and pests.
— Increased basal rate of respiration in plants.

Ultimate result of all the above factors will lead to *decrease in food production*.

• In temperate regions	Small increase in temperature may increase crop productivity slightly. — But higher temperature increase will reduce the crop productivity.
• In tropical and sub-tropical regions	Small increase in temperature will reducecrop productivity. — Rice production in South-east Asia will reduce by 5 per cent for every 1°C increase in temperature.

Inspite of the beneficial effects like CO_2 fertilisation effect, the overall effect of global warming would be that the total food or crop production of world would fall.

STRATEGIES TO REDUCE GLOBAL WARMING

Though the extent and exact effects of global warming are debatable, scientists generally agree that we should plan certain strategies to cut the emission of greenhouse gases. Some important strategies could be as mentioned below:

(i) *Reducing the use of fossil fuels* that we burn. We can make a big difference by improving the efficiency of heating systems and by reusing 'waste' heat from industry.
—Also we should develop alternative renewable sources of energy (like wind, water and solar energy).

(ii) *Increasing the forest and vegetation cover.* This would increase photosynthetic utilisation of CO_2. We should limit the felling of forests and use methods of agriculture that do not damage the land.

(iii) *Minimising the use of nitrogen fertilisers* in agriculture to reduce N_2O emission.

(iv) *Developing substitutes for chlorofluorocarbons* (CFCs).

DEPLETION OF OZONE

The greenhouse gases CFCs, CH_4 and N_2O rise up into the stratosphere and cause destruction of ozone. Most damaging effect is by CFCs, which are released from aerosl sprays, cooling agents, industrial solvents etc.

STRATOSPHERE OZONE DEPLETION

Formation of Ozone Layer (O_3) in Stratosphere

- In the stratosphere, the ultra violet (UV) radiations cause two processes to occur simultaneously, the destruction of ozone and the formation of ozone.
  - (i) Photodissociation of ozone into O_2 and O.
    $O_3 \rightleftharpoons O_2 + O$ (destruction of ozone)
  - (ii) O_2 and O quickly recombine to form O_3.
    $O_2 + O \rightleftharpoons O_3$ (formation of ozone)

The net result is that equilibrium is established and a *steady state of concentration of ozone layer is established.*

The Ozone Layer

- Ozone layer is present in the stratosphere between *20–26 km* above the sea level forming a shield over the earth.
- The thickness of this ozone layer, condensed to standard temperature and pressure averages varies at equator and at the poles.

Thickness of ozone layer at equator	0.29 cm
Thickness of ozone layer at poles	0.40 cm

- Concentration of ozone layer changes with seasons.

Concentration is higher	during February–April
Concentration is lowest	during July–October

- Ozone layer acts as a *protective shield*, the ozone shield. It absorbs the harmful UV radiations from reaching the earth. Absorption of UV radiation increases exponentially with the thickness of ozone layer.

  And so, since the thickness of ozone is more at poles, and

less at equator, less UV reaches the pole as compared to equator (or tropics).

Ozone Hole

The thickness of ozone is measured in Dobson Unit (DU).

1 Dobson unit (DU) = 1 part per billion (ppb)

Ozone thickness is decreasing every year.

- Ozone (O_3) thickness above Antarctica varied from 280–325 DU.

The thickness was sharply reduced to 225 DU in 1979 and 136 DU in 1985. It continued to decline to about 94 DU in 1994.

From 1956-1970	varied from 280–325 DU
1979	225 DU
1985	136 DU
1994	94 DU
1997–2001	reduced further by another 3 per cent approximately.

This decrease in the thickness of ozone layer in spring-time is known as ozone hole. The ozone hole was first discovered in 1985 over Antarctica.

Ozone is a different form of oxygen gas. The ozone thinning appeared for the first time in 1975. *The ozone hole is not a permanent feature*, but becomes evident each year for a few months during spring-time when it is Antarctic winter. Every September from 1975, the *ozone hole* reappears and each year the layer of ozone is thinner and the hole is larger. The existence of ozone hole was also confirmed above Arctic in 1990.

Ozone Hole

For decade NASA satellites have tracked the extent of ozone depletion over Antarctica. Every year since 1975 an 'ozone hole' appears in August when sunlight triggers chemical reactions in cold air trapped over the southpole over Antarctica winter. The hole intensifies during September before tailing off as temperature rise and in November and December.

In September 200, the ozone hole covered an area of 11.4 million square miles, 3 times the size of United States. It extended over the of city of Punta Arenas in Southern Chile with a population of about 120,000 people, exposing them to very high levels of UV radiation.

For making discoveries related to destruction of ozone layer, Sherwood Roland and Mario Molina, along with Paul Crutzen were awarded the Nobel Prize in 1995.

CAUSE OF OZONE DEPLETION

The gases CFCs, CH_4 and N_2O escape into the stratosphere and cause destruction of ozone (O_3). Out of these gases, CFCs are the major cause of depletion of ozone.

- CFCs rise up through the atmosphere and produce 'active chlorine' (Cl and ClO) radicals, which reduce Ozone (O_3) into Oxygen O_2. *CFC molecules can stay in the stratosphere for about 100 years.*
- *One chlorine atom from a CFC molecule could destroy 100,000 ozone molecules in the following mechanism.*
  - (i) UV radiation causes CFCs to release Cl atoms:

    $$CCl_3F \xrightarrow{UV} \boxed{Cl} + CCl_2F$$

  - (ii) UV radiations also act on O_2 to release oxygen free redicals.

    $$O_2 \longrightarrow \boxed{O}$$

    Cl atoms and O free radicals react with ozone to form oxygen:

    $$2\,\boxed{Cl} + 2O_3 \rightarrow 2ClO + 2O_2$$

    $$2ClO + 2\,\boxed{O} \rightarrow 2Cl + 2O_2$$

    Net reaction is $2O_3 \rightarrow 3O_2$ i.e., destruction of ozone molecules and converting ozone into oxygen.

CFCs have now been phased out in most countries of the world, but their effects continue, since CFC molecules can stay in the stratosphere for about 100 years.

So even if no more CFCs are put into air from tomorrow, the ozone layer will still take about 100 years to recover from the worst of the damage.

Methane (CH_4) and nitrous oxide (N_2O) also cause destruction of ozone through a series of complex reactions.

Effects of Ozone Depletion

The depletion of ozone layer leads to an increase in the UV-B radiation reaching the earth Surface. UV-B radiation is extremely harmful to living organisms.

- 5 per cent loss of ozone......It results in 10 per cent increase in UV-radiation.

Health Hazards

The ozone layer in the stratosphere forms the Earth's main shield against dangerous ultraviolet radiations from the Sun. This part of the spectrum, not detectable by the human eye, kills many forms of life such as bacteria and that is why it is used for sterilising surgical instruments and in protecting many foods.

Unfortunately, ultraviolet also kills and damages beneficial forms of life. If the ozone layer diminishes over populated areas—and there is an evidence that it has begun to do so—the consequences could be dire.

Middle and long wavelengths of UV cause not just tanning and sunburn, but the most prevalent forms of skin cancer. They also weaken the immune system which protects us from many harmful and even deadly diseases. Ultraviolet light has also been linked to eye cataracts.

According to a UN report, it has been estimated that:

- a 10 per cent loss of ozone would lead to an increase in the incidence of *non-melanoma skin cancer* by 26 per cent;
- increased UV-B radiation may lead to an increased incidence of melanomas, a more serious type of *skin cancer*;
- a 1 per cent decrease of ozone would lead to between 100,000 and 150,000 additional cases of *cataract-induced blindness* worldwide; and
- because skin pigmentation does not protect the body against changes in its *immune system*, experts foresee an increase of infectious diseases.

Other Effects of High UV-B Radiation

— Higher levels of UV-B radiation affect photosynthesis as well as damage nucleic acids in living organisms. UV-B radiation inhibits photosynthesis in most phytoplankton as it penetrates through the clear open ocean waters. This is turn affects the food chain of organisms that depend on phytoplankton.

PROTECTING THE ATMOSPHERE

The ozone layer, the fragile shield of gas which protects the Earth from the harmful rays of the Sun, is being damaged by chemicals released on the Earth. This carries serious risks for humanity. The ozone layer blocks out most of the sun's UV-B radiation—which causes skin cancer and cataracts in people, stunts plant growth and kills the tiny organisms which form the basis of the marine food chain.

The main chemicals involved in depleting stratospheric ozone are chlorofluorocarbons (CFCs), used in refrigeration, aerosols and as cleaners in many industries, and halons used in fire extinguishers.

The first evidence of damage came in the early 1980s, when scientists discovered a vast hole in the ozone layer above the Antarctic. Ozone-monitoring stations in Antarctica have detected average losses of 30–40 per cent in the total ozone layer region during the spring; at some altitudes the loss may be as high as 95 per cent.

Scientists estimate that if CFCs continue to be emitted as freely as they were in 1980, the ozone layer could be reduced by about 3 per cent during the next 70 years. Each 1 per cent reduction in ozone is likely to raise UV-13 radiation by about 2 per cent. Worldwide, this could lead to 100,000 more people going blind every year and 50,000 extra cases of non-melanoma skin cancer. Incidence of the most deadly form of skin cancer, melanoma, may also rise.

(*Source*: UNEP)

RISING OF SEA LEVEL

Causes of Rising of Sea Level

- Rise in sea level as a result of global warming is due to:
  - (i) Thermal expansion of ocean water,
  - (ii) Melting of glaciers and greenland ice sheets.

Implications of Sea-level Rise

(i) A rise of even half a metre (i.e. 0.5 m) of sea level would bring world's important cities and coastal areas under the threat of floods.

(ii) Since 1/3rd of human population lives within 60 km of a coastline, hence it would affect the humans tremendously.

(iii) Several low-lying islands may get submerged.

(iv) Coastal salt marshes and estuaries may disappear, and along with them would disappear the breeding grounds of a number of birds and fishes, leading to their extinction.

(v) Sea level rise will have negative impact on freshwater supplies, agricultural and dry lands, wet lands and on human settlement and fishers.

Is Sea Level Rising? By How Much?

Sea level is indeed rising. This determination is made when one sees changes in sea level over the entire globe for the past century. The Intergovernmental Panel on Climate Change (IPCC) has estimated that average sea level has risen 10 to 25 cm (4 to 10 inches) in the past century. However, sea level is affected by many factors, including local ones, such change at any single location may be either a rise, a fall, or no change.

Furthermore, IPCC estimates that sea level will rise 20 to 86 cm (8–34 inches) by the year 2100. In other words, sea level rise will not only occur in the next century, but will continue at an accelerated rate.

Do we have to Worry About It? Implications of Sea Rising Etamined

Given the above effects of sea level rise on human property, state and local governments have implemented certain policies to mitigate against the risk. *Setbacks* are zones along the coast which are at high risk of erosion. Property owners may not build or may have restrictions on building within these zones. These Zones are typically established for a certain time period into the future based on the current rate of erosion. For example, the 30 year setback is the zone of coast that is expected to erode within the next thirty years (i.e., 30 time the current annual rate of erosion). The purpose of setbacks is to allow the natural features of coast such as dunes, beaches and wetlands to migrate landward as sea level rises.

Setbacks, however, are unpopular with property owners because they impose restrictions. Therefore, some states have implemented a policy of *rolling easements* where owners may build but are required to remove a structure when it becomes threatened by an eroding shoreline.

Flood insurance costs will also rise. According to *FEMA*, a 30 cm (1 foot) rise in sea level is expected to increase flood damages by 36–58 per cent. As a result, insurance companies will have to increase flood insurance rates for coasts prone to flooding.

Often, the very engineering efforts built by humans to protect against sea level rise cause even more erosion. For example, the wave action at a bulkhead may prevent beach sediment from settling, so the sediment is deposited offshore rather than at the beach. Thus, the bulkhead works to enhance beach erosion rather than protecting against it.

Evolution of a Marsh as Sea Level Rises

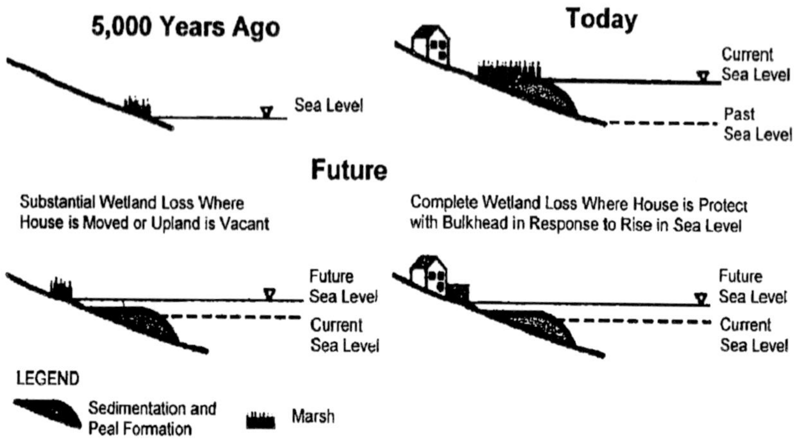

Fig. 5.8: Coastal marshes have kept pace with the slow rate of sea level rise that has characterised the last 50 thousand years.

The area of marsh has expanded over time as new lands have been inundated the future, sea level rises faster than the ability of the marsh to keep pace, the marsh area will contract. Construction of bulkheads to protect economic development may prevent new marsh from forming and result in a total loss of marsh in some areas

Furthermore, human engineering of rivers have interrupted the supply of sediment to coasts. For example, dams and reservoirs on rivers trap sediment and prevent the sediment from being transported to the coast. Wetlands on the coast, for example, grow vertically because the marsh grasses trap the sediment brought there by rivers. Under ordinary circumstances, many marshes would thereby maintain their elevation in the face of rising sea level. With the sediment supply from rivers cut off due to trapping of sediment in reservoirs, the marshes erode or become inundated because there is not enough sediment to be marsh.

Sea level rise also increases the risk of coastal areas to flooding. The higher the sea level, the higher the flood level of a storm. The *Federal Emergency Management Agency (FEMA)* has estimated that a rise in sea level of one foot would increase the size of the 100-year foodplain in the US from 19,500 square miles in 1990 to 23,000 square miles.

Water supplies for human or agricultural consumption are also affected by sea level rise. A higher sea level can mean that salty water intrudes into the underground coastal aquifers more often than if the sea level were lower. Also salty water can intrude higher upstream in estuaries, where the salty water may enter industrial or agricultural water intakes.

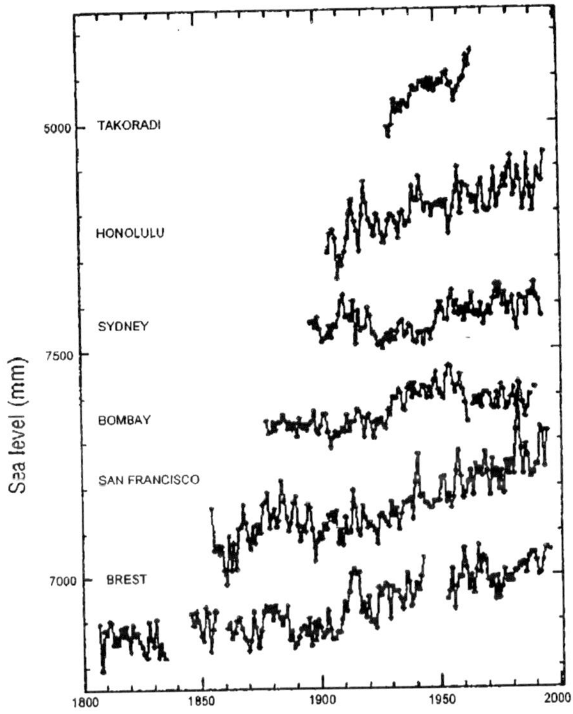

Fig. 5.9: Long Sea Level Records from Each Continent
Takoradi, Ghana (Africa), Hon Sydney (Australia), Bombay (Asia), San Francisco (USA) and Brest (Europe). Each been offset vertically for presentation purposes. Observed trends for the twentieth or 1.5, 0.8, 0.9, 2.0 and 1.3 mm/year respectively.

Source: *IPCC*, 1995, *Second Asse The Science of Climate Change*, Cambridge Univ. Press

What Causes Sea Level to Rise?

Much of the rise in sea level has been due to the rise in global temperature associated with the global warming of the past century. This type of sea level rise is known as *ecstatic sea level rise*. As the global temperature increases ocean water expands. This is also known as *thermal expansion* of the ocean water. The *IPCC* has estimated that thermal expansion has contributed 2–7 cm (1 to 3 inches) to the total sea-level rise over the past century.

In addition, as global temperatures rise, mountain glaciers melt. The IPCC estimates that 2 to 5 cm (1 to 2 inches) of the total sea-level rise over the last century has been due to the melting of glaciers. All over the world, scientists have documented the retreat of mountain glaciers, including the Rocky Mountains of North America, the Alps of Europe, and the Himalayas of Asia.

The effect of global temperature rise on the polar ice caps can be different at each of the two poles. Ice at the poles is of two types: *Sea ice*, or frozen water floating on top of ocean water, and *ice sheets*, or large masses of frozen water on top of large land areas. The large continental ice sheets are those on Antartica and Greenland. Whether these ice sheets are contributing to sea-level rise is largely unknown, but scientists are attempting to answer this question. It is hypothesised that Antarctica will not contribute to sea-level rise because it is too cold there. In fact, if the rise in global temperature increases global precipitation rates, Antarctica is expected to store water as snow and ice rather than contribute meltwater to the oceans. However, as ocean temperatures increase, the ice shelves around Antarctica may melt. While this may not contribute to sea-level rise (the ice shelves are already buoyant on the water's surface), the loss of the shelves may make the continental ice sheet unstable. Most scientists agree, however, that the Antarctic ice sheet will not pose a problem within the next century. On the other hand, it is hypothesised that the Greenland ice sheet will gradually melt and will contribute its water to the oceans, adding to the rate of sea-level rise.

Thus, ecstatic sea level rise is a combination of thermal expansion of ocean water, melting of mountain glaciers, and the possible melting of continental ice sheets such as those of Greenland.

Another factor contributing to the rise in sea level is the movement of land. Because the continents are dynamic and float on the Earth's mantle, continents exhibit their own movements over long time periods. So, if a continent or portion of a continent is rising, the ocean water at the continent's coast will appear to fall with respect to the motion of the land. Likewise, if a continent or portion of a continent is sinking, the sea level at the coast will appear to rise. This effect is known as *relative sea level rise*.

A continent can be rising as a result of a retreating ice sheet from a previous ice age. As the Earth warms after an ice age and the weight of the ice is removed, the continent rebounds or rises higher in the mantel. This is currently owning the last ice age. On this coast, sea level is falling, not rising.

A continent can also be sinking as a result of retreat of ice sheets after an ice age. During an ice age, as the ice-sheet presses down on the land, the land around the edge of the ice is forced up. When the ice sheets retreat, this land subsides. This is currently occurring in the Mid-Atlantic portion of the United States east coast. For example, in the Chesapeake Bay, the combined effects of sinking land (with its associated relative sea level rise) and ecstatic sea level rise are resulting in a rate of sea level rise that is twice the world average.

Land can also subside as the result of groundwater extraction. Human beings use groundwater for household and industrial purposes and obtain this water from aquifers deep within the ground. As the water is removed over long time periods, the land sinks. This is occurring in northern Italy where human beings have extracted groundwater for many decades. As a result, the city of Venice is threatened by rising sea level due to land subsidence as well as the eustatic rise in sea level.

How does Rising Sea Level Affect Us?

Rising sea level has such consequences as coastal erosion, increased flood risk and salt-water intrusion. Both human development and natural habitats are at risk when sea level rises.

Erosion is the main process that occurs to land as sea level rises. As a result structures built by peole will be destroyed by the sea as the shoreline retreats. Entire properties can be eroded away. In some areas, a 30 cm (1 foot) rise in sea level can result in 4500 cm (150 feet) of landward erosion.

Natural landforms such as dunes, beaches and wetlands are also at risk. Ordinarily, as sea level rises, these features migrate inland. However, human development often prevents this natural migration. Structures such as dikes keep new beaches or wetlands from forming behind them. As a result, the existing beaches and wetlands erode or become inundated with water. Organisms that depend on the habitat for such resources as food or breeding grounds will loose their habitat and be faced with fewer and fewer resources.

Source: NASA Global Change Master Directory Learning Center (2004) rising Sea Level ? Do we have to worry about it?

ACID RAIN

Meaning and Forms of Acids Rain

Acid rain refers to the deposition of acids from the atmosphere on to earth (Fig. 5.10).

— The oxides of sulphur (SO_2 sulphur dioxide, SO_3 sulphur trioxide) and oxides of nitrogen (NO_2 nitrous oxide, NO_2 nitrogen dioxide) are generated during the combustion of coal and gas in the industries and petrol in the automobiles.

— These gases being highly reactive, form secondary pollutants in air. They rapidly oxidise to form sulphuric acid and nitric acid and particles of nitrates and sulphates which quickly dissolve in water to form *acid rain.*

— These chemicals reach the surface of earth in two forms.

(i) *Wet Deposition.* It refers to *acidic water* received through rain, fog and snow. Sulphuric acid and nitric acid, formed in atmosphere dissolve in rain water and form dilute solution of sulphuric acid and nitric acid respectively. The rain carrying these acid is called acid rain.

Unpolluted rain is slightly acidic and has a pH of about 5–6 because of CO_2 that occurs naturally in the atmosphere. CO_2 combines with water to form a weak acid. Hence rain water is slightly acidic with pH of 5.6 to 6.5.

Rainwater in industrialised countries has a pH of 4 or below due to acid rain. In certain cities the pH of rain has been recorded as low as 2.3 (the some acidity as lemon juice).

(ii) *Dry deposition.* It refers to *wind blown acidic gases* and *acidic particles* in the atmosphere that settle down on the ground.

— It has been observed that 50 per cent of the acidity in the atmosphere is deposited on the earth as dry deposition.

— The dry deposited particles can also get washed from trees and other surfaces by rainfall.

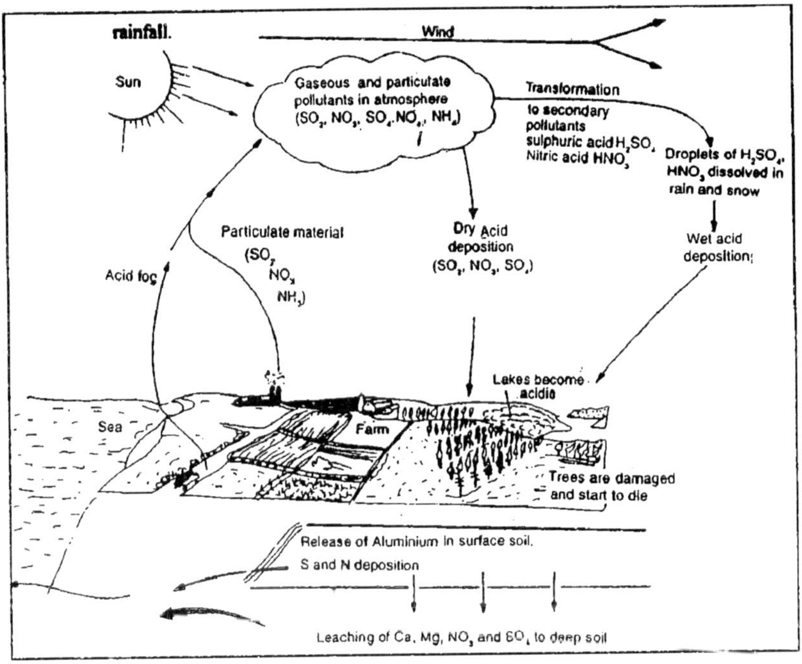

Fig. 5.10: Dry and Wet Acid Deposition or Acid Rain

Effects of Acid Rain

(i) Acid rain causes *severe damage* to monuments, buildings and statues. The acids in rain cause *corrosion* of the marble or brick surface. *Many historical monuments like Taj Mahal at Agra are being damaged by acid rain. For this reason only, the industrial units near the monuments are being shifted.*

(ii) Acid rain makes the *soil acidic*. This causes gradual degradation of soil and decline in forest and crop productivity. Low pH damages the soil microorganisms.

(iii) Acid rain causes *irritation* of eyes in human beings.

(iv) Acid rain is poisonous to plant life, fishes and aquatic animals. Most planktons, molluscs and fishes cannot tolerate water having pH below 5.0.

POLAR MELTING AT ANTARCTICA

While the ice shelves around the continent, such as the Ross Ice Shelf, are floating on the ocean, huge amounts of ice cover Antarctica.

If all of this ice melted it would raise global sea levels by about 200 feet. But climate scientists don't expect anything like this to happen in the next couple of centuries, if ever.

Antarctica is so cold that even the worst possible warming isn't likely to melt its ice for centuries. Still, there are concerns about what could happen to the West Antarctic Ice Sheet, which in theory could collapse into the sea to melt.

Except for Greenland's Ice Cap, the Arctic's ice is floating in the ocean. If it melted, it wouldn't raise sea level although it would have other effects on the world's climate.

REPORT OF THE WORKING GROUP OF THE INTERGOVERNMENTAL PANEL ON CLIMATIC CHANGE (IPCC, 2001)

The group consisting of experts from around the world that looked at the basic science of climate change made the following observations as regards its impact on the 21st century:

- Northern Hemisphere snow cover and sea-ice extent are projected to decrease further.
- Glaciers and ice caps are projected to continue their widespread retreat during the 21st century.
- The Antarctic ice sheet is likely to gain mass because of greater precipitation, while the Greenland ice sheet is likely to lose mass because the increase in runoff will exceed the precipitation increase.
- Concerns have been expressed about the stability of the West Antarctic ice sheet because it is grounded below sea level. However, loss of grounded ice leading to substantial sea level rise from this source is now widely agreed to be very unlikely during the 21st century.
- Global mean sea level is projected to rise by 0.09 to 0.88 meters (0.29 to 2.88 feet) between 1990 and 2100.

According to Jack Williams, "The idea that the polar ice caps are going to melt and flood the world sometime soon is a gross oversimplification.

INTERNATIONAL INITIATIVES FOR MITIGATING GLOBAL CHANGE

It is extremely important to lower and stabilise the concentration of greenhouse gases to save the earth from their harmful effects. For this the following agreements were signed by various countries.

1. *Montreal Protocol.* A landmark international agreement in 1987, signed by 27 industrialised countries.
   - It aims to protect the stratospheric ozone by agreeing to:
     - — limit the production and use of ozone-depleting substances,
     - — phasing out of ozone-depleting substances and
     - — helping the developing countries to implement the use of alternative to CFCs.
   - So far more than 175 countries have signed the Monotreal Protocol.
2. The United Nations Conference on Environment and Development.

UNCED Earth Summit

- It was held at Rio de Janerio, Brazil in 1992.
- It established the principles for reducing greenhouse gas emission.

3. *The Kyoto Protocol.* It was held in Kyoto, Japan during December 1997.
   - — It specified the commitments of different countries to mitigate climate change.
   - — This protocol requires countries to take appropriate measures to reduce their overall greenhouse gas emissions to a level at least 5 per cent below the 1990 level by the commitment period 2008–2012.

LOCAL ENVIRONMENTAL HAZARDS

All the elements mentioned under environmental pollution for example polluting gases like nitrogen dioxide (NO_2), carbon monoxide (CO) etc., and insecticides, cause changes in the local environment and hence are called *local hazards*. (For details see earlier chapter).

In today's industrialised world, these local hazards tend to take the shape of global hazards as they affect the environment of earth globally.

IMPORTANT POINTS

- All the pollutants ultimately find their way to the ocean water which is also getting polluted by oil spillage. It kills most of the plants and animals.
- Industrial *effluents* contain poisonous chemicals that lead to slow poisoning, unpleasant taste, odour etc.
- *Thermal pollution* is caused by release of hot water from the industries that causes death of flora and fauna.
- Polluted water causes a number of diseases. Excess of fertilisers or nutrients leads to eutrophication in lakes which ultimately kills most of the animals life.
- Water pollution can be controlled by treating the sewage before being discharged into rivers or oceans, recycling of pollutants and by treatment of industrial effluents.
- *Soil pollution* could be due to direct dumping of industrial wastes, agrochemical or discarded wastes or indirect by acid rain or other pollutants seeping into the deeper layers of soil.
- *Soil pollution* is mainly due to domestic solid waste, plastic *papers*, metals etc. It can be controlled by treating wastes in special waste disposal plants and by recycling certain materials like paper, plastic and metals.
- *Noise pollution* could be by any unwanted *high pitched sound* from machines, vehicles, blasting, domestic gadgets, even music and from supersonic planes. It causes physiological and psychological disturbances.
- *Radioactive pollution* is by testing of nuclear weapons, establishment of nuclear power plants and other uses of radiation.
- The radioactive substances find their way through nuclear wastes and coolants discharged in soil, through accidents or through food chain.
- A slight increase or prolonged exposure can lead to mutations, cancer and leukemia. It affects all the parts of the living organism.
- The strict enforcement of safety measures, banning of nuclear weapons and safe disposal of nuclear waste can help to control the radioactive pollution.
- Greenhouse gases like CO_2, CH_4, CFC and N_2O lead to global warming. But excessive increase in the concentration of these gases results in enhanced *greenhouse effect* which may

have following possible effects:

(i) CO_2 fertilisation effect on plants
(ii) Global warming
(iii) Depletion of ozone layer in the stratosphere

- Effects of global warming are:
  (i) Warming up of troposphere and cooling of stratosphere.
  (ii) Winter precipitation may increase at lower latitudes (like equator); but at higher latitudes, it is expected to increase in both summer and winter.
  (iii) Frequency of extreme events like floods, droughts may increase.
  (iv) Rise in see level.
  (v) Increased eruption of plant diseases and large scale death of trees.
- Global warming can be reduced by limiting the use of greenhouse gases, increasing forest cover, minimising nitrogen fertiliser and developing substitutes for CFCs.
- Ozone layer occurs in the stratosphere between 20–26 km above sea level. Ozone protects the earth by absorbing harmful UV radiations.
- Ozone hole has been appearing over Antarctica since 1985 every year in spring time (when its winter in Antartical). Its existence is confirmed over Arctic also.
- CFCs, CH_4, N_2O, mainly CFCs are the causes of depletion of ozone larger.
- In the absence of ozone shield, UV-B radiations that reach earth, cause damage to nucleic acids in living organism and increase the incidence of cataract and skin cancer and decrease immunity.

KEY TERMS

Acid rain	Oxides of nitrogen and sulphur in the air dissolve in rain water to form nitric acid and sulphuric acid. Rain carrying these acids is called acid rain.
Algae bloom	Excess or profuse proliferation of algae in water bodies.
Anthropogenic pollution	Refers to pollution caused by man.

Biodegradable	:	Pollutants that can be broken down by the activity of micro-organisms and enter the biochemical cycles.
Biological magnification	:	A phenomenon by which harmful chemical pollutants (normally non-biodegradable) get accumulated in the tissues in increasing concentrations as they travel along the food chain.
Black-foot disease	:	A disease due to chronic exposure to arsenic.
BOD	:	Biochemical oxygen demand. More BOD level in water means high microbial pollution.
Brown air (brown haze)	:	Refers to reddish brown haze caused by photochemical smog. Occurs in areas with intense solar radiation.
Carboxyhaemoglobin	:	A poisonous compound formed by carbon monoxide (CO).
Carcinogenic agents	:	The agents that cause cancer.
CFCs	:	Chloro fluoro carbons. They act as coolants, or as propellant gases for spray cans. They destroy the ozone layer.
CO_2 fertilisation effect	:	Response of plants to the increased concentration of CO_2 in the atmosphere. Results in increased rate of photosynthesis and increased growth in C_3 plants.
Deforestation	:	Cutting of forests.
Eutrophication	:	Sudden increase in nutrients in a lake leading to the algal bloom (profuse algal growth). This causes reduction in O_2 in water and leads to sudden death of fishes and other animals in water.
Fluorsis	:	Abnormal calcification of bones and teeth.
Global warming	:	Increase in the global mean temperature.
Greenhouse effect	:	Phenomenon by which CO_2 and other

		atmospheric gases like CH_4, N_2O and CFCs reflect the outgoing long wave infrared radiation back to earth, thereby warming the earth's surface.
Greenhouse flux	:	Refers to downward flux of infra-red radiation.
Greenhouse gases	:	Gases like CO_2 and methane that trap the heat radiated from earth and lead to increase in earth's temperature.
Grey air	:	Refers to grey haze or smog occurring in areas with less solar intensity.
Incineration		Combustion of wastes at very high temperature in the presence of oxygen.
Land degradation		Loss of land or soil due to human activities like overgrazing, deforestation, over exploitation, poor management etc.
Methaemo-globinemia	:	A condition in which excess nitrates from drinking water combine with haemoglobin to form non-functional methaemoglobin that impairs oxygen transport. Also known as blue baby syndrome.
Methanogens	:	Group of bacteria that decompose under anaerobic condition and produce methane gas as a product.
Methemoglobin	:	Nitrates from drinking water react with haemoglobin in the body to form methaemoglobin which is non-functional and hence reduces oxygen transport in the body.
Non-biodegradable	:	Pollutants that cannot be broken down to simpler and harmless products.
Oil spill	:	Accidental discharge of petroleum in oceans or estuaries.
Ozone hole		Refers to the decline in ozone layer thickness in August-September (spring time) leading to formation of hole in ozone layer.

Pollutant	:	Substances present in the environment in concentrations that are harmful to the environment and to the living organisms. Substances that cause pollution.
Pollution	:	At undesirable change in the physical, chemical and biological characteristics of our air, land or water. Caused by excessive accumulation of pollutants.
Pyrolysis	:	Combustion of wastes at high temperature in the absence of oxygen.
Radiatively active gases	:	same as green house gases.
Radio nuclides	:	Atomic nuclei of radio active substances like U^{238}, Th^{232} and C_{14}.
Skeletal fluorosis	:	A disease due to consumption of excess fluoride in drinking water. Hardened bones and painful stiff joints.
Smog	:	An irritant fog produced by the combination of smoke and water vapours.
Thermal pollution	:	Pollution by the release of hot water from nuclear plants or industries into water bodies.

Abbreviated Terms/Words

CO	:	Carbon monoxide
DDT	:	Dichloro diphenyl trichloro ethane
CFCs	:	Chloro fluoro carbons
UV	:	Ultra violet
COHb	:	Carboxyhaemoglobin
O_3	:	Ozone
PAN	:	Peroxy acetyl nitrate
VOC	:	Volatile organic carbon
NOx	:	Nitrogen oxides
COD	:	Chemical oxygen demand
dB	:	decibel
DU	:	Dobson unit.

6

Role of School in Environmental Conservation and Sustainable Development

SUPREME COURT DIRECTIVE ON THE COMPULSORY TEACHING OF ENVIRONMENT

On a public litigation petition, in 1991, the Supreme Court of India asked the NCERT and other concerned authorities to take steps to enforce compulsory education on environment in a graded way from the academic Session 1992–93. Since the order was not implemented even after eleven years, advocate M.C. Mehta filed an application to ensure implementation of the earlier order. The Supreme Court passed the order on April 22, 2004 for compliance.

The Supreme Court issued a notice on July 13, 2004 to the concerned authorities to inform it whether they had implemented orders for inclusion of environment as a subject in the institutions under their court.

It may be recalled that on April 22, 2004, the Court had endorsed a model syllabus prepared by the National Council of Educational Research and Training (NCERT) for introducing environmental studies as a compulsory subject from class one to class twelve.

The NCERT asked to be a model agency to monitor the implementation of the model syllabus in schools. The syllabus has been prepared after consultation with several experts and institutions, State Governments, the Central Pollution Control Board and Non-Government Organisations.

NATIONAL POLICY ON EDUCATION—NPE (1986 AND AS AMENDED IN 1992) ON ENVIRONMENT

In Part VIII entitled 'Reorienting the Content and Process of Education,' the NPE under the caption 'Education and Environment,' in Para 8.15 states, "There is a paramount need to create a consciousness of the environment. It must permeate all ages and all sections of society, beginning with the child. Environmental consciousness should inform teaching in schools and colleges. This aspect will be integrated in the entire educational process."

INTER-RELATIONSHIP OF POPULATION, ENVIRONMENT AND DEVELOPMENT

Population and Environment

Human population in the world is increasing at an enormous rate. It is estimated to become double in next 35 years. The population of India has already crossed 100 crore. If the current rate continues, it would not only lead to depletion of natural resources but also cause a number of socio-economic problems.

The impact of population explosion is clearly visible in many areas.

(i) It has led to encroachment on forests, mountains, seas and rivers and hence depletion of natural resources.
(ii) More people means more land required for living, cultivation and for grazing of cattle etc.
(iii) It has led to indiscriminate killing of animals for food.
(iv) The increased demand for timber and fuel wood has led to cutting down of trees and has made many places barren.
(v) Construction of roads, dams, urbanisation, more land for agriculture, all have led to deforestation causing ecological balance on earth.
(vi) Above all it has caused over-crowding leading to physical discomfort, mental tension and several socio-economic problems.

If it remains unchecked, it can be disastrous for human race.

ENVIRONMENT AND SUSTAINABLE DEVELOPMENT

Earlier man had limited needs and so he led a harmonious life with nature. With the advancement of science and technology, man has tried to manipulate the environment according to his needs, comfort and security. His needs have changed and the natural environment is shaped, and directed by socio-economic consideration. It has caused depletion and degration of natural resources.

Changes that have occurred in the natural environment are as under:

1. Old villages, hills, beaches and agricultural lands have been converted into cities and big towns.
2. For communication, a network of roads and transport has been established in villages as well as urban areas.
3. Importance to tourism had led to construction of big hotels occupying large areas.
4. Agricultural lands have been used to construct big hotels and industries.
5. To generate electricity for industries and large population, big dams have been constructed.
6. Conversion of forests into croplands or for human settlement has taken place.
7. Shrinking of water bodies has occurred.

Sustainable Development

The continuous increase in population and rapid development in the last century have imposed excessive demand on natural resources. There is a need to maintain a balance between the environment and development.

The need is to increase the production that is essential but at the same time to protect the environment and conserve the resources for future generation. This can be achieved by *sustainable development.* Conservation, sustainability and biological diversity are all inter-related. Sustainable development aims at harmony of man with nature and the practices that reduce dependance or use of natural resources. It can be achieved by various means like:

- Planting of more trees.
- Having more green grassy patches interspersed between concrete buildings.
- Adoption of technologies that are based on maximising the recycling of materials.
- Makeing judicious and efficient use of natural resources.
- Adoption of environmental friendly techniques like crop rotation, mixed cropping, biofertilisers and manures etc.

CONSERVATION AND PROTECTION OF ENVIRONMENT

Various activities of man have led to the depletion and degradation of natural resources. For man's own survival it is now important to conserve and protect the environment.

Conservation of environment means the activities that allow individual or commercial benefits but not the excessive use, leading to environmental damage.

Conservation can also be defined as the management and use of the biosphere in such a way that it provides greatest benefit to the *present generation* but also maintains its potential for the future generation.

Protection of environment means maintaining the nature as it is or as it might have been before the intervention of human beings or natural forces.

PRACTICES THAT HELP IN CONSERVATION AND PROTECTION OF ENVIRONMENT

1. Judicious use of fertilisers, intensive cropping, proper drainage and irrigation.
2. Composting organic solid waste for use as manure.
3. Rotation of crops.
4. Planting of trees in place of those removed for various purposes.
5. Establising national parks and conservation of forests by the Government.
6. Treatment of sewage, so that it does not pollute the rivers and other water bodies.
7. Harvesting of rain water.

ROLE OF THE SCHOOL IN ENVIRONMENTAL CONSERVATION AND DEVELOPMENT

In order to help students develop knowledge, skills, attitudes and values relevant to conservation and sustainable development, schools have to take up new roles and responsibilities. Teachers are expected to be not only the dispensers of knowledge, information, but also managers of teaching-learning situations. The entire school organisation, management and also classroom organisation have also to be suitably changed to meet the new challenges of environmental concerns and sustainable development.

The school is expected to discharge the following functions in relation to the conservation issues and sustainable development.

1. Developing awareness about environmental issues.
2. Providing specific and scientific knowledge topic-wise.
3. Organising conferences, group discussions and seminars.
4. Organising community surveys on issues relating to conservation and protection of environment.
5. Organising Social Service and Community service programmes.
6. Organising 'Population Days' and 'Environmental Days.'
7. Organising 'Awareness campaigns.'
8. Organising visits to pollution Control Centres.
9. Organising exhibitions on Environmental pollution and control.
10. Organising tree plantation or *Vanmahotsavs*.
11. Organising lectures and workshops for the benefit of the community.
12. Developing habits of cleanliness among students.
13. Ensuring cleanliness of the school plant.
14. Arranging lectures of experts on environmental issues.
15. Impressing upon students to adopt the following ways of protecting and improving the environment.
    - Dispose the wastes after separating them into biodegradable and non-biodegradable waste material.
    - Start a compost heap or use a compost bin. This can be used to recycle waste food and other biodegradable materials.
    - Send their waste oil, old batteries and used tyres to a garage for recycling or safe disposal; all these can cause serious pollution.
    - Never put any left over chemicals, used oils down the drain, toilet or dump them on the ground or in water or burn them in the garden. If it is done, it will cause pollution.
    - Don't burn any waste, especially plastics, as the smoke may contain polluting gases.
    - Reuse carrier bags.
    - Use unleaded petrol and alternate sources of energy, and keep the engine properly tuned and serviced and

the tyres inflated to the right pressure, so that vehicle runs efficiently.

- Avoid fast starts and sudden braking of automobiles.
- Walk or cycle where it is safe to do so. Walking and cycling can help to keep you fit.
- Use public transport wherever it is possible, or form a car pool for everyday travel.
- Avoid unnecessary or wasteful packaging of products.
- Plant trees. They will help to absorb excess carbon dioxide.
- Observe World Environment Day on 5th June.

Role of the Teachers in Environmental Conservation and Sustainable Development

All teachers in the school are expected to play a significant role in environmental conservation and sustainable development as these issues are closely related to national development. They should take due interest in all programmes in this respect. However, a special responsibility rests with those teachers who teach this subject. They should:

1. select, develop and implement curricular materials which will effectively make learners aware of:
   (a) how man's cultural activities (religious, economic, political, social, etc.) influence the environment from an ecological perspective,
   (b) how individual behaviours impact on the environment from an ecological perspective,
   (c) a wide variety of local, regional, national and international environmental issues and the ecological and cultural implications of these issues,
   (d) the possible alternative solutions available for remediating discrete environmental issues and ecological and cultural implications of these alternative solutions,
   (e) the need for environmental issues' investigation and evaluation as a prerequisite to sound decision-making,
   (f) the roles played by differing human values in environmental issues and the need for personal values clarification as an integral part of environmental decision-making,

2. utilise current theories of knowledge, attitude and behaviour relationships in selecting, developing and implementing a balanced curriculum which maximises the probability to desired behaviour changes in learners;
3. Adopt current theories of learning in selecting, developing and implementing curricular materials and teaching strategies to effectively achieve environmental education goals;
4. apply the theory of transfer of learning in selecting, developing and implementing curricular materials and strategies to insure that learned knowledge, attitudes and cognitive skills are transferred to life style decision-making by learners;
5. select effective instructional methodologies which are appropriate for desired cognitive and effective outcomes, characteristics of learners and existing classroom conditions;
6. effectively infuse appropriate environmental education curricula and methods into all disciplines to which the teacher is assigned;
7. effectively evaluate environmental education curricular methods and learners' achievement in both cognitive and effective domains;
8. take positive environmental action for the purpose of achieving and maintaining a dynamic equilibrium between quality of life and the quality of environment, and to develop, select, and implement curricular materials and strategies to develop similar competencies in learners to take individual or group action when appropriate;
9. investigate environmental issues and evaluate alternative solutions and to develop, select and implement curricular materials and strategies which will develop similar competencies in learners, including:
   (i) the knowledge and skills needed to identify and investigate issues, using both primary and secondary sources of information and to synthesise the data gathered,
   (ii) the ability to analyse environmental issues and the associated value perspectives with respect to their ecological and cultural implication,
   (iii) the ability to identify alternative solutions for discrete issues and the value perspectives associated with these solutions,

(iv) the ability to autonomously evaluate alternative solutions and associated value perspectives for discrete environmental issues with respect to their cultural and ecological implications,

(v) the ability to identify and clarify their own value positions related to discrete environmental issues and their associated solutions.

(vi) the ability to evaluate, clarify, and change their own value position in light of new information,

Practical Work and Project Activities To Be Undertaken by the School for Environmental Conservation and Sustainable Development

1. Preparing charts showing common flora and fauna in the neighbourhood.
2. Arranging trips to a wildlife sanctuary and Zoo.
3. Writing observations about local environment and vegetation.
4. Organising debates and discussions on topics related to various aspects of environmental conservation and sustainable development.
5. Preparing posters on river pollution, local water pollution, noise pollution.
6. Preparing posters on the consequences of deforestation.
7. Preparing posters on global warning.
8. Preparing posters on soil erosion.
9. Identification of plant protection chemicals.
10. Organising debates and discussions on population and its effect on environment.
11. Organising debates and discussions on the relationship between values and environment.
12. Organising surveys of the areas regarding environmental status in the locality.
13. Organising quizes.
14. Conducting simple practicals on environmental related issues.
15. Keeping the school plant clean.
16. Organising exhibitions on environmental related issues.
17. Arranging lectures of experts on environmental related issues.
18. Maintaining scrap books on environmental related issues.